THE
RACERS

HOW AN OUTCAST DRIVER, AN AMERICAN HEIRESS, AND A LEGENDARY CAR CHALLENGED HITLER'S BEST

NEAL BASCOMB

SCHOLASTIC
FOCUS

NEW YORK

Library of Congress Cataloging-in-Publication Data

Names: Bascomb, Neal, author.

Title: The racers : how an outcast driver, an American heiress, and a legendary car challenged Hitler's best / Neal Bascomb.

Description: First edition. | New York : Scholastic Focus, 2020. | Includes bibliographical references and index. | Audience: Ages 12 and up. | Audience: Grades 10-12. | Summary: "In the years before World War II, Adolf Hitler wanted to prove the greatness of the Third Reich in everything from track and field to motorsports. The Nazis poured money into the development of new race cars, and Mercedes-Benz came out with a stable of supercharged automobiles called Silver Arrows. Their drivers dominated the sensational world of European Grand Prix racing and saluted Hitler on their many returns home with victory. As the Third Reich stripped Jews of their rights and began their march toward war, one driver, René Dreyfus, a 32-year-old Frenchman of Jewish heritage who had enjoyed some early successes on the racing circuit, was barred from driving on any German or Italian race teams, which fielded the best in class, due to the rise of Hitler and Benito Mussolini. So it was that in 1937, Lucy Schell, an American heiress and top Monte Carlo Rally driver, needed a racer for a new team she was creating to take on Germany's Silver Arrows. Sensing untapped potential in Dreyfus, she funded the development of a nimble tiger of a new car built by a little-known French manufacturer called Delahaye. As the nations of Europe marched ever closer to war, Schell and Dreyfus faced down Hitler's top drivers, and the world held its breath in anticipation, waiting to see who would triumph"— Provided by publisher.

Identifiers: LCCN 2019059286 (print) | LCCN 2019059287 (ebook) | ISBN 9781338277418 (hardcover) | ISBN 9781338277425 (ebk)

Subjects: LCSH: Automobile racing—Europe—History—20th century—Juvenile literature. | Automobile racing drivers—Europe—20th century—Biography—Juvenile literature. | Grand Prix racing—History—20th century—Juvenile literature. | Antisemitism in sports—Europe—History—Juvenile literature.

Classification: LCC GV1029.15 .B37 2020 (print) | LCC GV1029.15 (ebook) | DDC 796.72092--dc23

LC record available at https://lccn.loc.gov/2019059286

LC ebook record available at https://lccn.loc.gov/2019059287

For Charlotte and Julia,
May you embrace life's fearful joys

PROLOGUE

"We Will Write the History Now"

The beast, long lurking in plain sight while the Allies stood idle, pounced at last. On May 10, 1940, wave after wave of German bombers, their engines in high pitch, swept across the dawn sky while armored columns rumbled overland. Into Belgium, Holland, and Luxembourg the Nazis advanced, shattering the morning quiet. Their paratroopers severed communication lines and captured essential bridges. Commandos dropped from glider planes and seized critical fortresses before they could stall any advance. In short order, panzer tank divisions barreled deep into foreign territory.

Within days, the Nazi spearhead, supported by artillery barrages and aerial attacks, crossed the Meuse River in France, forcing the Allies to retreat. By May 15, the French prime minister, Paul Reynaud, despaired over the telephone to his British counterpart, Winston Churchill, that the war was lost.

The French had some fight left in them, but they were, at best, panicked going up against what one witness called "a cruel machine in perfect condition, organized, disciplined, all-powerful."

At the news of the Germans' rapid advance, Parisians took

flight, particularly from the nicest quarters of the city. Railway stations were crowded with passengers desperate for tickets on sold-out trains, while overstuffed cars and buses jammed the roads leading south from the city. At the same time, refugees from Belgium poured into Paris from the north. "With bicycles and bundles and battered suitcases, holding twisted birdcages, and dogs in stiff arms," observed *Life* magazine, "they came and came and came."

Fearing an invasion for more than a year, the French had safeguarded many of their finest treasures. In Paris, monuments were sandbagged, and the stained-glass windows of Sainte-Chapelle had been removed. Curators at the Louvre emptied its walls of masterpieces such as the *Mona Lisa* and its floors of priceless sculptures. Convoys of nondescript trucks hauled these artworks to chateaus across the country. Likewise, French physicists evacuated their supplies of heavy water and uranium, instrumental to the pursuit of a nuclear bomb. Priceless art and rare substances were not the only items squirreled away as the German blitzkrieg threatened Paris. Across the city, people stashed family heirlooms in cellars and buried them wrapped in oilcloth. One Parisian hid a batch of diamonds in a jar of congealed lard that he left on his pantry shelf.

In an automobile factory on the rue du Banquier, in the working-class heart of the city, stood four Delahaye 145 race cars. The manufacturer's production chief intended to see his creations secured away, whether by dismantling them into parts, hiding them in caves outside the city, or, like those diamonds in the lard, masking them in the open, their engines and chassis covered up with new bodies—or none at all—and their true provenance concealed. These masterpieces could not be lost in the rage of war, nor found by the Nazis. There was little doubt that Hitler wanted them seized and destroyed for their temerity in challenging the Third Reich's famed Silver Arrow race cars, foremost those driven by their champions Rudi Caracciola and Bernd Rosemeyer.

In late May, the German army wheeled toward Paris. Prime Minister Reynaud exhorted his countrymen to fight to the death to hold the Somme, while his feckless war committee debated where to move the government when Paris fell. His staff collected secret papers to be sunk in barges in the Seine or burned in ministry yards.

Then, on June 3, the Luftwaffe hit Paris. Likened by one child to a "swarm of bees," Stuka planes dropped over a thousand bombs, targeting most intensely the Renault and Citroën factories in western Paris, which had transitioned to war production, much as their German counterparts, most notably Daimler-Benz and Auto Union, had done years before. The attack killed 254 and wounded triple that number.

The exodus from Paris accelerated.

Two days later, the Germans launched the second half of their campaign to take France. At the Somme, they ruptured the French line, their panzer divisions overpowering the courageous but doomed army. The door to Paris was ajar, and Reynaud and his government abandoned the capital.

Onward the Wehrmacht pressed.

In the capital, the growing numbers of routed French soldiers signaled the inevitable. Finally, on June 14, motorized columns of the German army—including heavy trucks, armored vehicles, motorcycles with sidecars, and tanks—entered an undefended city. Soldiers clad in gray and green followed on foot. The streets were so empty before them that at one intersection a herd of untethered cows aimlessly wandered past.

By the afternoon, swastikas flew from the Arc de Triomphe and the ministry of foreign affairs. An enormous banner was strung to the Eiffel Tower that read, in block letters, DEUTSCHLAND SIEGT AN ALLEN FRONTEN ("Germany is everywhere victorious"). Trucks fitted with loudspeakers threaded throughout the city streets, demanding obedience and warning that any hostile act against the Third Reich's troops would be punishable by execution.

On the Place de la Concorde, the German army commandeered the famously elegant Hôtel de Crillon and its neighboring colonnaded mansion, which was owned by the Automobile Club de France (the ACF). Founded in 1895, and the first such club of its kind, the ACF organized the French Grand Prix. Its membership included some of the wealthiest, most influential men in the city. Spread out over 100,000 square feet in a pair of buildings constructed during the reign of Louis XV, the club's quarters were well suited to its prestige.

One day early in the occupation, a Gestapo officer accompanied by several subordinates strode through the arched entryway of the ACF. The club's mahogany-paneled bars, its private bedrooms, and its shaded terraces were of no interest to him. Neither was he there to dine in one of its chandeliered, gold-trimmed restaurants, nor to swim in its palatial pool surrounded with statues like a Roman bath. Instead, the officer headed straight to the library, a cavernous, book-filled space that also held the ACF archives, with records of every race held in the country since

1895. They were an invaluable and unique resource, chronicling remarkable French wins and ignoble defeats alike.

"Bring me all the race files," the Nazi ordered the young ACF librarian. The voluminous records were boxed up and brought out on a cart. While his subordinates hauled them away, the Gestapo officer turned to the librarian. "Go home and never return here, or you'll be arrested. We will write the history now."

The tale of René Dreyfus, his odd little Delahaye race car, and their champion, Lucy Schell, was one of the stories that Hitler would have liked struck from the books.

This is its telling.

THE
RACERS

PART I

THE DREAM

CHAPTER 1

Just one more check. René Dreyfus circled his Bugatti Brescia again. At five feet, seven inches tall with the wiry build of a jockey, René weighed no more than 140 pounds dripping wet. An oversize cap, loose slacks, and suit jacket added to the impression of a young man lost on his way to a neighborhood dance. He sported a nonstop smile and had brown eyes alight with what one journalist labeled The Look: "a stare of searing intensity and undying affection that let you know, without a doubt, René was put on earth to drive cars fast."

Aged only twenty, he needed his mother's written permission before he was allowed to take part in the race—the La Turbie hill climb—on February 25, 1926. Under a cloudless blue sky, the young man from Nice squeezed himself into the wicker seat.

Preparing to crank the engine into life was his brother, Maurice, the Brescia's co-owner and René's ride-along mechanic. René turned the fuel-line knob, then pressured the tank with four strokes of the fuel pump to his left. *Ready*, he nodded to Maurice. A jerk of the crank, and the Brescia's four-cylinder, 1.5-liter engine** jarred into life with a *blaaaaaatttt . . .*

....

** Very generally the bigger the engine, the more power it produces.

blaaaaatttt . . . blaaaaaattt. Maurice climbed into the open cockpit beside his brother, as blue oil smoke sputtered from the exhaust pipe.

The race officials waved them toward the slightly inclined start position. Blocks of wood were placed behind their rear tires to keep them from rolling backward when René let go of the clutch.

A young René Dreyfus.

Pressing down on the accelerator, he roused the engine into a throaty *rrrrrraap . . . rrrrrraaaappp . . . rrrrraaaaaaapppppp.* More blue smoke cast a pall over the road behind him. Eyes fixed on the starter flag, he curled his fingers on the steering wheel and angled his body forward. A nervous shiver ran through his body. Maurice gripped the windshield frame. Getting away quick was everything.

The starter raised the flag. The race would take mere minutes and would be over before René's nerves calmed. The flag snapped downward. René punched the accelerator as he released the clutch. The Brescia surged ahead, up toward the first sharp turn.

Considered the father of all hill climbs, the course ran along the Grand Corniche, a road built by Napoleon that twisted like a serpent through the mountains along the French Riviera to an altitude of 1,775 feet. The route was famous for its gradients, cliffs, ravines, and twists, and ended at the charming hilltop village of La Turbie. The low stone barrier along the cliff edge offered slight comfort.

René accelerated out of the bend at Mont Gros, by the domed Nice Observatory. If Maurice bellowed at him to slow down, he did not hear him over the engine's bark. There were no other cars against which to measure himself. It was the best time that won. Hundredths of a second could determine the winner. He must race at the extreme, testing his mettle, and the Brescia's too.

Into the next hairpin, René shifted down into second gear. He and Maurice were sandwiched together as they went into the turn. Coming out of it, he accelerated, the *rrraaaappppp-rrrrrraapppppppppp* of the Brescia echoing across the jagged mountains. There were a couple hundred feet until the next bend. There was no point in saving his engine or worrying about his tires. The race was too short.

René knew every bend, hollow, turn, and rise on the course. He knew precisely where to angle the front wheels into a corner, exactly how far to allow the Brescia to drift for the following turn, and the best gear for every point on the road. Finally, the course flattened out. Ahead, they saw a crowd of ladies in dresses and gentlemen in suits lining the road, children sitting at their feet. The finish. René left nothing in the engine as he shot across the line, a whirl of dust and gravel behind him.

The clock read 5 minutes 26.4 seconds, an average of 43 miles per hour (mph), or 69.2 kilometers per hour (kph). It was a very fast time—the fastest ever at La Turbie in his small-engine class. Now he had to wait for the others. By early afternoon, all the competitors had finished. René had clocked the sixth-fastest time and was first in his category, beating his nearest rival by almost a minute and a half. Rousing congratulations, a shiny medal, and a celebratory dinner were his rewards for his biggest win yet.

These were all very nice, but René was impatient to be a *professional* race-car driver. There was nothing more he wanted from life.

When he was a boy, his father, Alfred, occasionally allowed him to stand between his knees and hold the steering wheel of the family's Clément-Bayard, a colossal car. One time, René convinced his brother and sister and his sister's friend to join him in his two-seater pedal car on a ride down their hometown's longest hill. The four were already shooting down the hill when they realized that the tiny handbrake could not slow the weight of four children moving at velocity. To avoid plunging into the river at the bottom of the hill, René swung the wheel to the left, flipping the cart over. Maurice threw up everywhere; the girls were traumatized. René thought it a thrill.

War against Germany broke the idyll of René's childhood in 1914. Alfred was drafted into the French army, and as Kaiser Wilhelm's troops advanced into France, his wife, Clelia, and their three children had to flee their home in Mantes-la-Jolie, just outside Paris.

In Nice, and later Vesoul, the young family waited for Alfred to return from the war, which he did. After the armistice, the family returned to Paris, and Alfred's business—raincoats and fine garments—blossomed. But he was in poor health. Although he had survived several gas attacks during the war, his lungs never fully recovered.

In 1923, when René was eighteen, the Dreyfus family returned to Nice, now a thriving cosmopolitan city with all the bohemian culture of Paris but better weather, overlooking azure-blue waters. Shortly after the move, Alfred died of a heart attack. René felt unmoored.

The family sold their house and moved into an apartment. Alfred had invested in a paper business for his sons to work in, and they bought a two-seater, 6-horsepower (hp) Mathis for René to travel about Nice and nearby towns, selling paper. On the winding, treacherous roads outside Nice, René schooled himself in how to drive fast. He loved the euphoria he experienced being in tune with the Mathis as it careered through the hills.

He entered his first race in 1924, the Circuit de Gattières, forging his mother's name to do so. His eighty-year-old grandfather helped him fit a huge exhaust pipe to the Mathis and strip off the fenders so that it qualified for its category. Maurice rode aboard as mechanic, always the protective brother. Uncontested in his small-engine class, René won the race.

He was convinced he needed a Bugatti so he could enter more important races, and the local Bugatti dealer, Ernest Friderich, was only too happy to sell a Brescia to another young man with glory in his eyes.

Maurice Dreyfus and his father, Alfred, in the Mathis, the first car René ever raced.

After his grandson's triumph at the 1926 La Turbie hill climb, René's grandfather delicately clipped out any mentions from the Nice newspapers and glued them into a large scrapbook, taking care to note the publication name and the date in his fine handwriting.

CHAPTER 2

Over the next few years, the pages of the scrapbook filled with cuttings about René's wins and places in hill climbs and provincial races across the Riviera, and the shelves in his bedroom filled with medals and trophies. Friderich the Bugatti dealer took René under his wing and managed his race schedule in return for a split of his winnings.

René had yet to earn any income from his racing, but he was a dominating presence in local events. And he was keen to move out of the little leagues. In 1929, Friderich secured René a spot in the inaugural Monaco Grand Prix, but the young driver was piloting an outdated, underpowered Bugatti and barely ranked. Over the next year, he competed on an almost weekly basis, supported by his family and Friderich, pushing for the race that would catapult him into the big time.

Every season, the AIACR Sports Commission, which represented racing-car manufacturers including Mercedes, Alfa Romeo, Maserati, and Bugatti, as well as the various national automobile clubs of Europe, determined a formula to which cars and races had to adhere if they wanted to be part of the official Grand Prix circuit.

This stipulated the length of the race, the cars' engine size, design, weight, and dimensions, and what types of fuel were allowed—all to enforce some degree of uniformity and to level the playing field. Among the events, there were Les Grandes Épreuves like the French and Italian Grands Prix, which earned drivers points toward the European Championship as well as two dozen other races. Teams also participated in sports-car races. Separate from the Grand Prix, where cars were basically stripped-down bullets, these races required vehicles to be fitted with lights, fenders, and other road equipment that would be found on a typical highway. A win at some of these events, including the Targa Florio, 24 Hours of Le Mans, and Mille Miglia, were coveted the same as a Grand Prix triumph. Then there were the hill climbs like La Turbie and endurance contests like the Monte Carlo Rally.

At last the Monaco Grand Prix came around again. On the night of April 2, 1930, René was awake in his hotel room, wrestling with doubts over his chances in the upcoming race. He should have been asleep—he needed the rest. In only its second year, the "Race of a Thousand Corners," so called because of its sinuous 1.97-mile course through the hillside heart of Monte Carlo, was the world's most glamorous "round-the-houses" circuit, and its one hundred laps were a true test bed for drivers and their cars.

The month before, René and Friderich had taken the leap and purchased a 2.3-liter Type 35B Bugatti, fitted with a supercharger.** René entered two small races with his new car and

----

** By drawing compressed air and fuel into the engine's cylinders, a supercharger allows more fuel to be pumped into each chamber, creating a bigger explosion when the mixture is ignited by the spark plugs and thus more power from the piston stroke.

won both. He felt like a "child with a new and better toy."

Just before dawn, René came up with an idea. His car had a 26.5-gallon tank, which would require refueling after sixty laps. If he added an extra tank, then he could skip the pits and save a couple of minutes. It could make the difference that gave him a top finish.

Still in his pajamas, he hurried down the landing to his manager's room. Groggy and irritated, Friderich answered the door. "Come on, we have some work to do," René said before rattling out his idea.

Friderich stared at the enthusiastic René, two decades his junior. Then he said, "Good night. I'm going back to bed." René pushed into the room. He only needed a nine-gallon tank. "Where'll we put it?" Friderich asked. "On a trailer?"

"No, no, in the cockpit . . . on the seat . . . under a canvas. No one will see it." René didn't think of the risk of jostling a tank of gas beside him on the passenger seat.

"It won't work," Friderich said. "The tank will just be dead weight. It will get in your way. You'll need to stop anyway, to clean your googles, to get a drink of water."

No tank, no race, René threatened. None of the rules forbade it.

The two woke up Maurice to mediate the standoff. Finally, Friderich backed down: "It's you who's driving." The three men went to the garage to figure out how to make it work.

Early the next morning, René drank a coffee, ate a croissant, then went down to the pits on the promenade. The rising sun glittered off the Mediterranean. He and Friderich double-checked everything on the car, from the engine down to their special preparations for the second tank. Afterward, René took a walk to calm his nerves.

Monaco's small population had mushroomed in anticipation of the race, and spectators gathered everywhere: in the grandstands; on hotel terraces; aboard yachts, fishing vessels, and dinghies jamming the harbor; across the hillsides of the "Rock of Monaco" where the prince's palace stood; and on rooftops and along every foot of the course, which had been fortified with low walls of sandbags. At certain points, onlookers could almost stretch out and graze the cars with their fingers, an immediacy René found intoxicating.

He returned to the pits and shared some cold chicken and Bordeaux wine with Maurice under the shade of a palm tree. Then officials waved at the drivers to bring their cars into their places. These had been drawn earlier by lottery, and René was in the fourth row. There were seventeen competitors, and given the tight course, early positioning was critical.

As tradition had dictated since the inaugural Gordon Bennett Cup in 1900, the cars were painted in colors based on their driver or team's nationality: blue for French; white for German; red for Italian; green for British; and yellow for Belgian.

René made one last check of his car, then knelt to make sure his shoelaces were triple-knotted. Once, a loop on his laces had caught on the clutch, and he had nearly driven into a wall. He folded himself into the cockpit and took a sip from the long straw sunk into a thermos of iced cola.

Friderich came up to him: "Don't force too much at the beginning. Wait until the twentieth lap. Then your engine will be warm." René nodded. Then he was alone. He adjusted his white cloth helmet and goggles and tried to settle down. Pandemonium surrounded him: the static squeal of the loudspeakers, the music from the band, the spectators in the grandstands, the sudden churning of engines. He tried to force it all from his mind.

The starter, Charles Faroux, raised a single finger, alerting the drivers that it was one minute until the start. The editor of *L'Auto*, France's preeminent sporting newspaper, and founding director of the 24 Hours of Le Mans, Faroux was the ringleader of French motor racing. Wearing his trademark straw hat and an elegant suit, he raised the red-and-white Monégasque flag above his head, then swept it down.

With a blast of sound, seventeen cars bolted wheel to wheel down the promenade toward the right-hand cambered curve before Sainte-Dévote Chapel. Coming out of the bend, René shifted into third gear to ascend Avenue de Monte Carlo.

Louis Chiron's Bugatti was already in the lead. René was far in the back, but there was no room to pass in the "multicolored serpent" of cars shooting up the 600-yard inclined straight at 93 mph. He glanced at his tachometer, which measured the speed of the engine: 5,300 revolutions per minute (rpm). *Hold back*, he thought. *Save the cold engine.* At a slight bend in the climb, he punched down to first gear, his path blocked by a yellow Bugatti and a monolithic white Mercedes. Then it was back up to

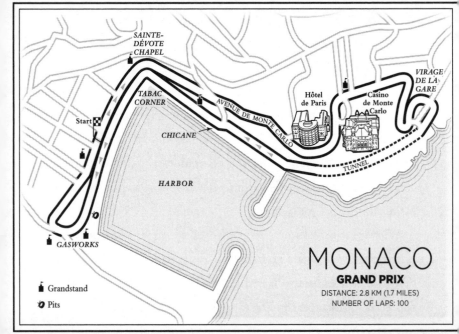

Map of Monaco course.

second, then third. He considered fourth, then came back down through the gears.

At the top of the straight, now high above the water on the city's cliffsides, he banked left alongside the Hôtel de Paris, then drove through the manicured gardens in front of the Casino de Monte Carlo. Then he tore down a short straight followed by the three hairpin bends in succession—right—left—right—as he descended into a "dive into a dull, stone-side ravine" to the railway station. There were moments during those narrow turns when mere inches separated the nose of his Bugatti from the car in front.

Another right curve at the water led into a 130-yard tunnel lit by flickering arc lights. As René accelerated through the soft, long curve, the bellow of the engines in the arched stone tunnel reverberated inside his skull. Any errant tug at his wheel, and his Bugatti would crash against the sides of the contained chute, tumble end over end, and he would be dead.

Out in the light again, he dashed down a short straight bordered with tamarisk trees, still at the back of the pack. A rapid left–right jog of the wheel brought him through the chicane, a designed curve in the road to slow drivers. Then he ran along the harbor, swung a left at Tabac Corner, sped beside the water's edge, past the pits, a hairpin at the gasworks, and was racing back toward the start.

Louis Chiron and William Grover-Williams, the 1929 winner, jockeyed for first with almost record lap times, while the Italian Luigi Arcangeli nipped at their heels in his Maserati.

René bided his time, moving up where he could. In the tenth lap, he broke into the middle of the pack, but he was almost a minute behind the leader, Chiron, who was already lapping competitors.

Cars had begun to fall out of the race. Count Max Arco-Zinneberg's huge 7.1-liter Mercedes SSK smacked into a pile of sandbags. Mario Borzacchini's Maserati hit a wall. Others experienced brake trouble or their engines seized up.

At twenty laps, René pushed into third place, but Chiron was a minute and a half ahead now. René kept to a fierce pace—sweat soaked his overalls, and he shifted gears almost continually, accelerating to 100 mph in fourth, then down to 10 mph in first. On average, there was a turn every twelve seconds. Throughout, he kept an eye on his fuel and oil gauges, switching valves and regulating the pressure with the hand pumps when needed. His arms ached, and his fingers and palms grew blistered and numb.

The blast of a cannon from a yacht in the harbor announced the halfway point. Only the durable Bugattis, ten in total, continued to run, but the crowd sensed it was a two-person contest between René and Chiron, who was still almost a whole lap ahead. With each round of the circuit, René nibbled seconds from his lead.

Shortly after the sixtieth lap, René's main tank was ebbing low, so he switched open the fuel line from the tank on the seat beside him. Gasoline flowed smoothly to the engine. He would not have to stop in the pits. Chiron would. René could barely see through his oil-slicked goggles. Stopping to clean them, to rest his hands, or to gather his breath would cost precious seconds. Now with the deadweight of the tank starting to lighten, he could go even faster, even more nimbly through the corners.

Finally, on lap 83, Chiron pulled into the pits. When René came into the harbor straight, he saw Maurice and Friderich jumping up and down on the sidelines. As he sped down the parallel straight, he spotted Chiron climbing the Avenue de Monte Carlo. He had spent fifty seconds refueling, and René was now only ten seconds behind. Within reach. Over the next two laps, he tightened contact.

Then he saw his opening in one of the hairpin turns in the descent to the tunnel. With a burst of speed, he seized his chance and, sliding out of the corner, claimed the lead. Three car lengths behind, Chiron ripped off his blue crash helmet and tossed it aside. Over the rest of the race, René increased the gap to twenty seconds and spent the time repeating to himself, "Be very careful now . . you *cannot* make a mistake . . you *are* going to win the Grand Prix of Monaco."

At the finish, Faroux waved the checkered flag, and a stampede from the pits encircled René. Friderich and Maurice embraced him, almost knocking heads together. Strangers clapped him on the shoulder and thanked him for their big payouts at the bookies.

A weary but victorious René Dreyfus and his sponsor, Ernest Friderich (on the left), after the 1930 Monaco Grand Prix.

René drank champagne and basked in the spotlight of his victory. Newspapers featured photos of his boyish face smudged with oil. Between his first-place prize and sponsorship bonuses, he earned a generous sum of almost 200,000 francs (roughly 150,000 US dollars in today's money).

Most important, he had claimed his first major Grand Prix.

CHAPTER 3

The concept of a self-propelled vehicle, without horse or ox, had always intrigued inventors and scientists. Leonardo da Vinci sketched plans, as did Isaac Newton. As far back as the sixteenth century, horseless carriages fitted with sails had maneuvered the roads outside Amsterdam. In the 1770s, Nicolas-Joseph Cugnot, a French military engineer, built a steam-powered tricycle to haul artillery. Sixty years later, in England, a steam carriage rolled along a country road at 12 mph. Farmers blocked its path with trees to prevent it from spooking their livestock.

The invention of the four-stroke internal-combustion engine changed everything. It was an invention with many fathers, but it was mastered by Gottlieb Daimler and Nikolaus Otto in Germany in 1876, when they gave the world a small, lightweight, efficient machine that converted power into motion. Ten years later, their countryman Karl Benz patented a gasoline-powered vehicle that boasted a one-cylinder, water-cooled engine, three wheels, a tubular frame, brakes, and buggy seats. The automobile had arrived.

Dozens of manufacturers sprang up across Europe and the United States. Initially, they produced a motley bunch of cars. The driver sat on an open-air bench, using a wobbly tiller to steer. The engine was housed in a high square box. Solid rubber covered wooden artillery wheels. A brake lever pressed a block of wood against the tires. A bulbous copper horn alerted pedestrians. The headlights were like lanterns.

The engines grew to two cylinders, then four, and beyond. An increase in speed followed. Pneumatic tires arrived as well as steering wheels, though at first, they were big enough to helm a yacht. Drum brakes replaced the blocks of wood. Mechanics were needed on board to operate the hand pumps and tubes feeding

A catalogue featuring the "Benz Patent Motor Car" with extras: removable half top and leather mud flap. Carl Benz has taken a seat himself.

lubricant oil and fuel to the huffing, puffing beast of an engine.

Maneuvering the first cars was no leisurely affair. It took strength, moxie, and, most of all, an ability to endure being "boiled from the waist down and froze from the waist up." Regardless, automobiles sparked the public's imagination.

As is human nature, drivers immediately began competing in town-to-town road races, which were spectacles attended by hundreds of thousands. First, Paris to Rouen. Then, Paris to Bordeaux, Marseille, Berlin, and farther afield. Before the races started, crowds mustered in the half-light of dawn around vehicles—De Dions, Panhards, Daimler Phoenixes, Peugeots, Delahayes, and Benzes—of every shape and size. The drivers wore heavy leather coats, goggles as big as snorkel masks, and thick gloves to protect their hands while steering these beasts.

There were no road signs. Few depots at which to refuel. No decent maps. Drivers sped through clouds of heavy brown dust, navigating by the telegraph poles that lined the road.

Competition fueled innovation. The first Mercedes, built by the Daimler company, marked advances in every aspect of the automobile: from engine efficiency, to suspension, chassis,** steering, and brakes. The car managed speeds of just over 50 mph. Piloted by Wilhelm Werner, the Mercedes beat all comers at one of its first competitions: the 1901 La Turbie hill climb.

Year by year, the cars—and the races—grew bigger and faster. And deadlier. Those willing to race were increasingly draped in riches and glory. The price might have been the risk of death, but it was worth it for the exhilaration of teetering at the edge of the impossible, the landscape passing in a fogged blur, the thrum of the engine melding with one's heartbeat.

Tragedy did, however, prompt race organizers, most notably the ACF (Automobile Club de France), to abandon open-road races for controlled circuits with guidelines that determined what kind of car could compete. In 1906, the ACF put together a race on a 64-mile triangular circuit protected by a palisade outside Le Mans, France. Only cars that weighed under a maximum of 2,200 pounds (1,000 kg) were allowed to enter the twelve-lap, two-day event. Hungarian Ferenc Szisz, driving a Renault, beat out thirty-one others to win a trophy and 45,000 francs in prize money. He also secured his place in history by winning the first-ever Grand Prix.

....

** The chassis is the framework of the vehicle.

CHAPTER 4

In lashing rain, on the south bend of the AVUS racetrack outside Berlin, Rudi Caracciola pulled his Mercedes to a halt. Moments before, during practice for the inaugural 1926 German Grand Prix, two cars had collided. The sight of the twisted wreckage sent a shudder through him as he climbed out of his seat to help.

Two emergency workers bundled Italian driver Luigi Platé into an ambulance, leaving his mechanic, Enrico Piroli, on the ground. Eyes open, he lay flat on his back, his arms and legs spread wide. Rain pelted his lifeless body and rolled like tears down his cheeks. While Rudi stared in disbelief at his first dead body, a paramedic draped a sheet over Piroli, leaving only his white canvas shoes sticking out. The test runs canceled, Rudi returned to his Berlin hotel. The sight of those muddied white shoes haunted him.

Rudi had always had an appetite for trouble, initially fostered at his family home, the Hotel Furstenberg in Remagen, by the Rhine in Germany. Before he was out of knee socks, he was known as the "King of the Rhine Valley Scoundrels," a suitable nickname for a boy with a noble bloodline that ran a thousand years back to roots in Italy, hence the non-German-sounding Caracciola.

He was fourteen when he lost his father in World War I, and his mother, Mathilde, was kept too busy running the family business to properly manage her son's rebellious streak. Rudi "borrowed" a guest's Mercedes before he was old enough to see over the dash—lurching forward, grinding the gears, nearly hurtling off the road. As a teen, he ran a bootleg wine operation and commandeered the hotel's yacht to charge passengers to cross the Rhine. His mother chalked up the incidents to high-spirited youth and got used to smoothing over the uproars that inevitably followed.

Rudi came of age during the era of the record-setting Blitzen Benz and the winning of the 1914 French Grand Prix, on the eve of war, by his countryman Christian Lautenschlager over Frenchman Georges Boillot. Just shy of six feet tall, Rudi was built like a spade, square-shouldered and slim-waisted. He had dark hair swept cleanly back from a high forehead above coal-colored eyes, a pug nose, and a square jaw.

Motorcars would always come first for him—before school and before running the hotel. His mother tried to convince him otherwise, but he did not waver. The family thought he might come around if he actually had to work in a grimy automobile factory. The mechanic's job they secured him at Fafnir in Aachen only heightened his enthusiasm, and he even had the chance to enter their cars in some races. Rudi found that the faster he drove, especially in competition, the calmer and more at ease he became. He struggled to find such peace in any other part of his life.

Later, he took a job at the Mercedes showroom in Dresden. Situated on the city's busiest, most fashionable street, the showroom easily attracted customers, but Rudi failed to make a single sale.

He spent most of his time gazing at the young ladies who stayed at the lavish European Hotel catty-corner to the showroom. One in particular, a beauty with cropped hair, dark eyes, and fair skin, caught his attention. A frequent guest at the hotel, she always took the same second-floor room and, on occasion, stood at the window, watching the passing traffic.

Rudi shared a few glances with her, once even a smile, but she was rarely alone. The hotel concierge told Rudi her name—Charlotte Liemann—and that she went by Charly. She was the daughter of a well-known Berlin restaurateur and married to her father's chief assistant. The fact that she was married failed to cool Rudi's passion.

One afternoon, he attended a dance at the hotel when Charly was in town. He asked her to dance, expecting another slow foxtrot, but the band switched into a fast tango, and he found himself lost in the thrill of being close to her.

"You're not very talkative," she said.

"I'd like you to watch me racing someday," Rudi blurted.

"Why?"

"Then you'd have more regard for me."

Charly chuckled, and the two left it at that.

Rudi continued to badger his bosses for a car to race; it didn't matter what the event. Finally, they lent him a touring car for a local event. A win brought more opportunities and faster cars. Between stints at the showroom, in his suit and starched white shirt, he traveled with the Mercedes team and participated in smaller races while the lead drivers, Christian Werner and Otto Merz, competed in the Grands Prix.

Every year, the big auto manufacturers, such as Bugatti, Alfa Romeo, and Mercedes, hired their drivers for the upcoming season. These drivers earned salaries and a cut of appearance money and prizes. They got to pilot the latest, most advanced cars and were supported by experienced crews. Team managers handled all the logistics of when and where they competed.

Usually, Rudi was little more than a hired hand, assigned to drive one of the trucks or a chassis without a body. But he also got to watch the greats at work, meet their technical director, Ferdinand Porsche, and join the postrace dinners. He spent most of his time with Alfred Neubauer, an Austrian driver several years his senior with whom he shared his hotel room on the road.

Over the course of 1926, Rudi's prowess as a driver earned him even more victories and further favor with Mercedes. But he was discontented. He wanted to compete in the fastest cars on the greatest stage of all: the Grand Prix. He approached Max Sailer, a former driver and now head of the Mercedes race department, with a proposition. He told Sailer that he wanted to represent Mercedes at AVUS, at the German Grand Prix. After being pestered for a couple of hours, Sailer relented— partly. He promised Rudi a car and a support team, but only if he took part as an independent. The company couldn't risk a mediocre showing by someone from the official team. Adolf Rosenberger, another skilled young driver, would participate under a similar arrangement.

Under a dark gray sky on Sunday, July 11, Rudi waited tensely at the line. In the seat beside him was his young mechanic, Eugen Salzer. The field was dense, with thirty-nine cars. Rudi's training runs at AVUS had gone poorly, and a half dozen other drivers had clocked much faster times. He continued to have visions of Piroli's body.

The starter whipped the flag downward, its snap lost in the growling thunder of revving engines. Rather than joining the cacophony, Rudi's engine stalled. "Quick, man!" he yelled at Salzer as his competitors sped off. "Give us a push!"

Salzer jumped from the cockpit and shoved the Mercedes from behind. Rudi released the clutch, and the engine kicked into life. The mechanic leaped back inside just before Rudi took off. Over a minute had passed.

Rudi tore down the six-mile straight at 100 mph, past a screen of pine trees, and into the sharp southern loop. "For God's sake, slow down!" Salzer cried, almost thrown from his seat. But Rudi only roared out of the curve, then back up the parallel straight, separated from the other by a thin patch of forlorn grass.

He feared that he had lost the race already but was determined to continue. He fought to make up the gap. By the third lap, he had closed to the middle of the pack. During lap 4, the drizzle turned into sweeping torrents of rain that soaked him to the bone and cut his visibility almost to nothing. He barely slowed over asphalt now slicked with rain and oil. His tires shot out plumes of water.

Cars began to withdraw from the race.

Coming into the northern bend in his seventh lap, Rudi spied the other white Mercedes, Rosenberger's, on its side, the time-keepers' booth smashed into toothpicks. He would later learn that Rosenberger had skidded out of control, and that two race officials were dead, a third grievously wounded.

When Rudi stopped in the pit for gas and oil, he asked Porsche if his teammate was okay. "Just slightly hurt," Porsche lied. Rosenberger and his mechanic had been hurried off in an ambulance. Rudi slung out of the pit, back into the race. On the opposite straight, French champion Jean Chassagne lost control of his Talbot, shot across the separating grass in front of Rudi, then rammed into the spectators.

One lap after the next followed. Rudi lost count. He passed car after car but had no idea of his position. At that time, there were no signals for drivers from the pit as they passed. Rain continued to pour from the sky, and Rudi drove through a haze of tension and exhaustion, Salzer urging him, "Faster!"

Finally, after twenty laps, 243 miles, and almost three hours of driving, he came into the finish, stopped, and lifted off his goggles. He was clueless as to where he had placed. His legs shook, almost as if they were lost without the need to shift, brake, or accelerate. People crowded around him, cheering. Even when they draped flowers over the steaming hood of his car, he could not believe it. He had won his first Grand Prix and with it the nickname "The Rainmaster."

1926 German Grand Prix winner Rudi Caracciola with his copilot, Eugen Salzer.

CHAPTER 5

After his first win at AVUS in 1926, Rudi became one of the top aces in Europe. He was rich and famous—and believed there could be no stopping his sweep of victories year after year for Mercedes. Then, one day, he found himself staring at a letter that had just been delivered. It was stamped with the star-and-laurel symbol of his team and dated November 1930. The letter was from Wilhelm Kissel, CEO of Daimler-Benz, Mercedes's parent company, and it stated that Rudi's contract would not be renewed in 1931. Mercedes was abandoning motor racing—the sport was too expensive.

The Wall Street crash the year before had sent ripples of destruction—economic and political—far beyond the shores of the United States. Germany was particularly hard hit. Banks shuttered. Financial panic stalled production. Exports dried up. Corner shops, farms, industrial firms, local governments—all went bankrupt.

Cushioned by his racing winnings and his own family fortune, Rudi had felt little effect from the crisis until now. He went to meet Kissel in his office at Daimler-Benz headquarters in Stuttgart. No matter what argument Rudi made, Kissel ticked off the reasons why racing was a luxury he could ill afford: a sharp drop in domestic sales; the dead export market; a labor force reduced by half; a sagging bottom line.

Defeated, Rudi left Kissel's office and went to see Alfred Neubauer, who was waiting with Charly, now Rudi's wife, in his nearby office. "It's finished," Rudi said. "All over."

Charly rose from her chair. "If you can't drive for Mercedes, then drive without them." Neubauer scowled. Charly suggested Alfa Romeo. Neubauer thought it ridiculous. Rudi was solemn. No matter what, he needed to race. It was everything.

Neubauer grew frantic. "But . . . you can't . . . It's like going over to the enemy. It's almost treason!"

"You can't expect me not to race, to give up my career?"

After Rudi and Charly departed, Neubauer, a force of nature on any given day, worked on Kissel. If running a team was too expensive, how about Rudi represented Mercedes independently? If investing in the development of a new car was too costly, why not allow Rudi to buy the latest SSK himself—at a discount, of course.

Neubauer had reinvented the role of team manager, not least with his system of flag signals and chalkboards that alerted a driver to his position against his competitors, the number of laps remaining, and when to come in for a pit stop. He was a master organizer with an elephantine memory for courses, drivers, and lap averages, and knew every car inside out. He volunteered to manage Rudi and secure a small staff. If the company funded their salaries and expenses, they would split any earnings with Rudi. Mercedes could not lose—and given that Rudi had won almost a dozen events in 1930 alone, they might come out ahead.

On April 12, 1931, the northern Italian town of Brescia was alive with the revving of homegrown engines: Itala, Bianchi, Maserati, Fiat, Alfa Romeo. Rudi's white Mercedes SSKL was one of the few challengers of foreign design. Ninety-eight cars shot down the road toward Cremona on the first stretch of the Mille Miglia—the Thousand Miles race.

Following a figure-eight course, with Bologna at its center point, the competitors—both amateurs and professionals—swooped down public roads as far south as Rome, then climbed north along the serrated spine of the Apennines back to Brescia. All along the route, from the biggest cities to the smallest hamlets, spectators came out to watch. Italy was crazy about motorsport, and the Mille Miglia was its national pride.

The route, raced night and day, was too long to scout in advance. It crossed through scores of villages, barren valleys, and nameless intersections. Only Italians, its organizers believed—and history had proven them right—could know more than a fraction of the often treacherous course or muster the support needed for such a long race. They clearly had never seen the likes of Alfred Neubauer. He had charted out every mile and set up rolling depots along the route.

Rudi had the power advantage in his Mercedes, and he barreled down the straights at over 120 mph. The Alfa Romeos, piloted by Italians Tazio Nuvolari and Giuseppe Campari, were not turtles to his hare, but Rudi gained an early lead and sustained it through the first 200 miles. South of Siena, darkness fell, and somewhere along the serpentine roads to Rome, Nuvolari overtook him and claimed first position.

Nuvolari was known by many nicknames, including "The Maestro" and "The Flying Mantuan." Such was his desire to dominate that he had once competed in a motorcycle race with two broken legs bound in plaster—and had won.

During the night, Rudi fell to sixth place, then farther back. Refusing to give up, he rallied and returned up the leaderboard. As dawn crested on the horizon, Rudi edged his SSKL to go faster. His Italian rivals tried to box him out on an open stretch of highway, but he overcame them. With 250 miles left, he did not look back, crushing his nearest challenger, Campari, to the finish by over eleven minutes. It was the first win in the Mille Miglia by a German driver, and a German car.

Shortly after Rudi's return from Italy, Kissel asked him a favor. They were late on the delivery of a custom Mercedes, and to smooth over any potential irritation of their very special Munich-based client, Kissel wanted his celebrity driver to make the delivery.

Rudi drove the 7.7-liter, black convertible Mercedes with bulletproof windows, steel-plated side panels, and glove compartment with a secret nook for a revolver, from Stuttgart to the Mercedes dealership in Munich. There the car was washed and polished to a shine, and Rudi changed into a nice suit and tie, all the better to make a good impression on the client: Adolf Hitler.

Accompanied by Jakob Werlin, the Munich Mercedes dealer, Rudi then drove the car to a grand stone mansion for the appointed hour of 5 p.m. A distinctive flag flew over the

Rudi and his wife, Charly, in their heyday, traveling the circuit.

building: a black hooked cross in a white circle on a field of red—
the swastika. Although Hitler's racist political ideas and violent
methods were well known, Rudi was curious, and not a little
eager, to meet the man who was a rising political force in
Germany.

Awaiting them on the steps of the building known as the
Brown House, the Nazi party's national headquarters, was
Hitler's private secretary, Rudolf Hess. Hess led Rudi and Werlin
into an expansive, high-ceilinged study where Herr Hitler was
seated at a desk. On the wall behind him was a life-size portrait

of Henry Ford. Hitler was a car enthusiast, and he greatly admired the American tycoon.

Rudi had seen numerous photographs of Hitler, but in the flesh the man was shorter and stockier than Rudi had imagined he would be. Hitler lavished praise on Rudi for the Mille Miglia win. What a victory for Germany! Before Rudi could respond, Hitler rattled a barrage of questions at him about Italy: How were its trains? What were the living conditions? Did people admire or loathe Mussolini?

Rudi made a joke about how little one could see at 100 mph, but Hitler pressed him for answers. He seemed uninterested in the brand-new Mercedes parked outside and instead gave Rudi and Werlin a tour of the Brown House. One of the trophies he showed them was the bloodstained banner from the Beer Hall Putsch in 1923, where the Nazis made their violent bid for power.

Later that day, Rudi chauffeured Hitler around Munich at a quiet pace, and the Nazi leader marveled at the car, calling it a true testament to German craftsmanship.

The whole experience made a deep impression on Rudi.

Although he had won the German Grand Prix and the Mille Miglia, Rudi and Mercedes soon parted ways. The worldwide financial depression continued, and sinking auto sales made any form of sponsorship, even a profit-sharing one like Rudi enjoyed in 1931, difficult to maintain.

Neubauer tried to keep Rudi in the star-and-laurel family, making promises about competing in the United States. Without any guarantees, and knowing that Mercedes would not invest in keeping up with other automakers, Rudi declined. "I've got to drive, don't you see," he told Neubauer, and he signed up with Alfa Romeo for the 1932 season.

After spending so much time in the Mercedes SSKL, a car he likened to a locomotive, Rudi could barely contain his joy the first time he drove an Alfa. "As light-footed as a ballerina," he said to its designer, Vittorio Jano, in praise of its handling. His new teammates, who included Tazio Nuvolari, were skeptical that the German could handle such an agile, featherweight car, but Rudi quickly proved them wrong.

In their crimson Alfa Romeo P3 *monopostos* ("single-seaters"), supercharged rockets on wheels, Rudi and the Flying Mantuan dominated the Grand Prix. Tazio won the French. Rudi claimed the German. He also triumphed at Monza and a host of smaller races and hill climbs. At the end of the season, he ranked second only to his teammate, who won the European Championship.

They were truly on top of the world.

CHAPTER 6

French reporter Jacques Marsillac arrived at the stylish Parisian restaurant ready for lunch. A distinguished correspondent who had covered uprisings in Ireland and North Africa, his new assignment was to accompany American heiress and rally driver Lucy O'Reilly Schell on her next adventure. Trench coat draped over his arm, he surveyed the lunchtime crowd.

A woman's voice rang out over the hubbub. "So what if their car went into the ditch four times?" it boomed in English. "Was that really a good reason to forfeit?" Thirty-five years old, thin, ruddy-faced, blue-eyed, and with bobbed auburn hair, Lucy Schell commanded the room. In fact, she commanded any room she occupied, all five feet, four inches of her, whether she was dressed in high fashion in a city restaurant or dressed in oil-stained overalls in a garage.

Her husband, Laury, to whom she had addressed her remark, did not protest. Laury was Lucy's opposite in every way—as reserved and quiet as she was lively and loquacious.

Lucy spotted the reporter across the restaurant. Her bright smile widened as she approached him, and in flawless French, she said, "At last! There you are! Come, I'll introduce you. We were talking about the Rally." Once seated at the table, Marsillac got an earful about what lay ahead in his role as "ballast" for the

Schells' car in the upcoming 1932 Monte Carlo Rally.

Launched in 1911, the Rally was a supreme test of endurance for its participants and their automobiles. Competitors started from their choice of more than a dozen far-flung places, including Stavanger in Norway; Gibraltar, off southern Spain; Athens, Greece; John o'Groats in the north of Scotland; and Palermo, in Sicily. The finish line was always in Monte Carlo. The greater the distance traveled, the greater the challenge and the higher the number of points to be earned by the drivers.

Drivers needed to reach control stations during a specific window of time to prove that they were maintaining an average speed of at least 25 mph. That speed seemed very slow to Marsillac, but Lucy explained how difficult it was to meet even that pace, given that there were no allowances made for sleeping, eating, refueling, repairs, poor navigation, or accidents.

The Schells planned to take the second-longest route, starting in Umeå, Sweden, one hundred miles from the Arctic Circle and some 2,300 miles from Monte Carlo. The journey would take four days and three nights, driving almost nonstop. Although he was no delicate flower, Marsillac was cowed by the thought of the adventure facing them, particularly when he heard about the icy road conditions.

When the teams arrived in Monaco, they would have to undertake a convoluted series of tests of their driving skills—and the reliability of their cars—to determine the winner.

A week after the lunch, at five in the morning, the Schells collected Marsillac at the offices of his newspaper, *Le Journal*. They appeared ready for a polar expedition—Lucy in a long waterproof jacket, wool trousers, and knee-high leather boots. When they met for lunch, Laury had looked to Marsillac like a sallow mortician. Now, wearing a heavy fur-lined coat and boots, he seemed a vigorous giant.

The Schells' black Bugatti Type 44 was similarly well fitted out, with fenders, spare tires lashed to its sides, and three headlights perched on a bar at the front. Inside, there was enough gear to mount a siege: food stores, mechanic tools, picks, shovels, rope, tire chains, and a block-and-tackle set that could lift the car out of a ditch. There was so much stuff that Marsillac had to burrow himself into a space on the back seat underneath a pile of luggage, blankets, and camera equipment. He was joined there by Hector Petit, winner of the 1931 Rally, who was catching a ride with them to the starting line in Umeå.

"When do we sleep?" asked Marsillac.

"When everyone is too tired to drive," Lucy answered from behind the wheel. When that happened, they would sleep in the car by the side of the road.

Lucy and Laury shared the driving equally. She was every bit as resilient as her husband—and a bit faster too.

After five days and nights, the Schells and their passengers were on the last leg of their journey. A number of competitors had already turned back, giving up even before the start of the race. One rallyer never had even that chance. While swerving to avoid an approaching horse-drawn sledge, he overturned his car and was killed.

Lucy Schell and her husband, Laury, at the Monte Carlo Rally

They were leaving Sundsvall, a couple hundred miles from Umeå. Lucy dozed in the back seat, Laury was driving, and Marsillac was navigator. It was dark, and a thick fog had settled over the road, which was covered with four inches of ice.

Seconds later, their tire chains lost their grip, and the car swung to the right. There was a brief moment when it seemed as if they were gliding through the air. Then they smacked into a bank of snow. When everyone inside had regained their wits, they realized that the car was tilted on its side and the slightest movement caused it to rock.

Carefully, the four crawled out and inspected the damage with flashlights. The car looked all right, but it was half buried in the snow and their winch insufficient to the task. It was 1 a.m., thirty below zero, and they were stuck in the middle of a pine forest at least a dozen miles from the nearest village.

Petit and Marsillac lumbered off in a biting wind to try to find a farmhouse and help. Lucy and Laury hacked at the hardened snow with their picks and shovels. One hour passed. Then two. Petit and Marsillac returned, having given up the search after they heard wolves in the woods. The Schells had barely made a dent in the snowbank, yet they carried on digging.

The question of whether they should abandon the race before the start, as others had done, was never even raised. This was just a normal day for the Schells. It was not the life that Lucy's parents had wanted for their daughter, but saying yes to Lucy and whatever she wanted was always a far cry easier than saying no.

The only child of exceptionally wealthy parents, Lucy had

received every advantage, to the point of being spoiled, although rather than settling her into indolence, this doting instilled in her a confidence to pursue her ambitions. Her father, Francis Patrick O'Reilly, was raised in Reading, Pennsylvania, the son of Irish immigrants who fled the Great Famine of the 1840s. He made a fortune, first in construction, then by investing in real estate and factories in his hometown. At the age of forty-six, he met and, in January 1896, married Henriette Celestine Roudet in her hometown of Brunoy, south of Paris. That October, Lucy Marie Jeanne O'Reilly sprang into the world.

Lucy spent her youth traveling between the United States and France. A biographer wrote: "While she grew up in the United States and absorbed its spirit of independence, she remained unmistakably Irish both in looks and temperament, combining a natural charm and vivacity with headstrong courage, obstinate determination, and a careless outspokenness." When asked the country for which she swore the most allegiance, she said, "I am American," but the briskness of her answer betrayed the feeling that she never felt completely at home anywhere. She was also decidedly nouveau riche and unapologetic about it.

She met and fell in love with Selim Lawrence (Laury) Schell, a diplomat's son whose American parents had settled a short distance from Brunoy. Laury had trained as an engineer but was uninterested in work, despite having only a meager inheritance. Lucy's father tried to dissuade her from the relationship, advising her, "His life seems to consist entirely of the pursuit of pleasure," but Lucy was not one to listen to advice.

During the early years of World War I, she worked as a nurse at a military hospital in Paris, caring for soldiers who had suffered every type of horror, particularly injuries from artillery shells: severed limbs, burns, disfigured faces, and shrapnel wounds. Their suffering was seared into her mind. In April 1915, a month after Zeppelins began bombing Paris, she and her mother, accompanied by Laury and his brother, left for the United States.

Interviewed by an American newspaper, Lucy railed against the calamity brought by the German invasion and thanked America for its aid. She promised that France was not yet defeated. "Even the most dangerously wounded soldiers as they lay on their beds of pain and tossed and moaned in delirium begged and prayed to be allowed to return to the front and fight for their beloved country."

Two years later, Lucy and Laury returned to France and got married. After the armistice, they lived in Paris, in a place and during a time that Ernest Hemingway famously described as "a moveable feast." The city bloomed with the talents of F. Scott Fitzgerald, Cole Porter, Ezra Pound, Coco Chanel, Man Ray, and Pablo Picasso. Lucy was one of the cadre of wealthy Americans fueling the party.

The births of her children—Harry in 1921 and Philippe five years later—failed to settle her down; rather, becoming a mother had the effect of revving her up further. A defining characteristic of the Roaring Twenties was a love of speed. Across Europe and the United States, the number of car races of every sort exploded: "flying kilometer" trials, hill climbs, circuit contests, and intercity rallies. Laury and Lucy were both drawn to the scene, first as spectators, then as drivers.

Thanks to Lucy's family's money, she could afford to buy the latest, and best, cars. And she could compete in those cars as well—if and when she was allowed. By the early 1930s, she was one of the top female drivers in Europe, racking up wins in a Bugatti 35, Talbot M67, and Alfa Romeo 6C. As for silver-spoon airs or a lack of toughness, she suffered from neither. Before one race, she broke her arm in several places, and her doctor told her to forfeit. She refused, participating with a thick plaster cast on her arm, and nearly won.

Her favorite event was the Monte Carlo Rally. In 1929, she ran it alone and placed eighth overall and first among the women. The following two years, she partnered with Laury. They always flew the Stars and Stripes, and year after year, they were the Rally's highest-placed Americans. In 1931, they placed third. This year, however, it looked like their race might be over before it had even begun.

Then, miraculously, two forest workers appeared down the remote road. They promised to return with help, and an hour later a truck fitted with a huge snowplow arrived. Another truck followed, carrying ten bearded Swedes wearing fur caps. They cleared away the snow underneath the Bugatti and hauled it free from the bank.

The rescued rallyers garbled thanks in pidgin Swedish, then started the car. The engine rumbled uneasily in the bracing cold but settled. They advanced again into the night, getting lost a few times over the last hundred miles to Umeå. One local barricaded his door when the Schells knocked to ask for directions, but most people generously pointed out the way.

CHAPTER 7

In the early hours of Saturday, January 16, 1932, the *pop-pop* of flashbulbs lit up the night in Umeå as photographers captured drivers speeding away. First was Louis Chiron, at 3:34 a.m. Then, at intervals, one marque after another followed him over the starting line: Riley, Sunbeam, Lagonda, Triumph, Ford, Studebaker, Chrysler. They were cheered on by a few hundred Swedes, most of whom had traveled long distances to get there, on skis or ice skates.

At last, a race official announced to No. 57, the Schells' Bugatti, "Two minutes, gentlemen." Lucy ignored the gentlemen. As soon as they had the signal to go, she made her start, driving steadily and slowly, in complete contrast to those who had torn away at full throttle.

The road was coated with a foot of ice, its surface glistening. A person could barely stand on it, let alone drive without spikes or military-grade tires. A Talbot swooped past them. Before it disappeared around a bend, its headlights danced left, then right. There was a sharp swish, almost like the sound of a boat breaking through a swell, and the lights were extinguished.

Lucy pulled up beside the car, which was stuck deep in a hollow beside the road. Its team waved—all okay—and Lucy drove on. Save in the case of injury, regulations forbade drivers helping other competitors. Despite several sideway lurches of their own into ditches, the Schells' car reached Sundsvall fifteen minutes before the cutoff time. At the control, located inside the town's fanciest hotel, they dashed off their signatures, ate some ham sandwiches, then started for Stockholm, 230 miles away.

A mix of rain, snow, sleet, and fog met them—and this on narrow roads through ravine-ridden countryside. From the back seat, Marsillac likened the jolting, back-and-forth movement across the road to being stuck inside a cocktail shaker.

They shared the road with local traffic: motorbuses, sledges, and sometimes families out on ice skates. Use of the brakes guaranteed an uncontrollable slide, but both Schells handled the Bugatti with supreme skill. They rarely slowed, allowing the wheels to glide across the ice to carry them around turns. Marsillac was particularly struck by how Lucy's smile widened, the tougher conditions became.

At 1:50 a.m. on Sunday, they arrived in Stockholm and took a brief break to stretch their legs and refuel at the depot. Then they were off again, cutting southwest across Sweden's pine forests. Over a dozen teams had already retired from the race.

Hour after hour of navigating these roads, able to see only a few yards ahead, wore down the drivers. At 6 a.m., a few hours before the Nordic sunrise, they decided to rest for a short spell. They parked the car by a barn and dozed off quickly, leaning against each other in the front seat. Marsillac squirmed about until he found a comfortable position in the back. Then—

With the clap of her hands, Lucy announced, "It's seven!

Quick, back to it." By their maps, they had over 150 miles to go to the ferry port at Helsingborg, where the last ferry to Denmark departed at 1:45 p.m. It was already past 9 a.m.

"We are not stopping again," Lucy declared. She whizzed at 40 mph along the axle-deep rutted roads that would have been better navigated at a crawl. As they neared the coast, she continually checked her watch. One hour until the ferry left.

Forty-five minutes.

Thirty minutes.

Fifteen.

She sighted Øresund Strait, then the ferry. The remaining competitors were already loaded on board, and plumes of black smoke were pumping from the ferry's stacks when the Bugatti came to a screeching halt by the gangplank. Lucy leaped from her seat, shouting, "Wait, Captain! Stop!"

They had made it.

The Danish roads were better, and the Schells and Marsillac reached Germany without any issues. At the border, they guzzled black coffee before speeding off toward Hamburg. From there, they turned toward Brussels, 375 miles away. Such was their exhaustion that it was a challenge to remember what country they were driving through. Over a week had passed since any of them had slept in a proper bed, bathed, or even removed their boots. When Marsillac went into a hotel to send a dispatch by telephone to his newspaper, the staff looked at him as if he were a beggar.

At this stage of the Rally, the term *endurance trial* took on a new meaning. When Lucy was not driving, she was taking care to ensure her husband stayed awake at the wheel. She pestered him with questions whenever she feared he might be drifting off. From Brussels, they journeyed 200 miles to the Paris checkpoint, arriving in the afternoon under dark gray clouds and a persistent drizzle. They needed to reach Monte Carlo the next day, between 10 a.m. and 4 p.m. Over 600 more miles to go.

The highway south of the French capital was a slippery mess. Lucy and Laury reduced their shifts to an hour each time, but their reactions at the wheel remained mushy. Their speech slurred; their eyes drooped asleep for tenths of seconds before wresting awake. No amount of wind from an open window, no amount of shaking their heads, no amount of clenching their fists could alleviate the weariness.

They continued down the poplar-lined roads, often through heavy downpours. Whenever Laury asked Lucy to rest, she would grumble that she was fine but would eventually give over the wheel. There were little mistakes: a bend taken too wide, a drift to the left, a missed turn. These piled up, but none of them resulted in an accident. Others were less fortunate. A Danish team, while fixing a broken headlight at the roadside, were struck and killed by another competitor blinded by the rain and his fogged-up windshield.

On Wednesday morning, they crossed over the mountains into Monaco. Rain pounded the pavement, and fog obscured the elegant terraces of Monte Carlo. When the Schells emerged from their Bugatti at the finish line, on schedule, they swaggered like conquering heroes. Only half the contingent from Sweden had made it.

After a short rest came the "flexibility test" to decide the winner. The team who traveled one hundred meters in the slowest time with their engine in top gear followed by one hundred meters in the quickest time would earn the most additional points. After many hard-fought miles, it was a farcical way to determine the victor, but that was the Rally.

Laury piloted the Bugatti during the test, Lucy beside him. She was so tense that she forgot to start her stopwatch. As the Bugatti puttered at 3 kph (1.86 mph) in fourth gear across the 100-meter stretch, she urged her husband to give the engine some gas, believing that it would surely stall otherwise. But Laury managed to crawl forward without incident. Then he turned in a semicircle, jammed on the gas, and sped back across the same distance.

A fellow starter from Umeå, Maurice Vasselle, driving a Hotchkiss, scored with the best times and claimed first place. The Schells finished seventh.

Caught up in the spirit of the Rally, and awed by Lucy Schell, Marsillac chronicled their adventures for all of Paris to read. His story shared the front page with news of a train derailment, another shake-up of the French cabinet, and a story about the German "nationalist leader" Hitler, who was promising that "only by his own strength" would Germany be great again. Secure from these troubles—for now—Lucy was already thinking of finding a new car, one equal to her ambition to be the first woman to win the Monte Carlo Rally.

Her timing was impeccable.

At the Delahaye automobile factory on 10 rue du Banquier, Paris, production chief Charles Weiffenbach was working through some papers in his office, when his secretary peeked in through the door to inform him that he had two visitors. They did not have an appointment but insisted on seeing him nonetheless.

"Their names?" Weiffenbach asked sternly. The lantern-jawed sixty-one-year-old looked like a general who had misplaced his uniform.

"The Schells: Lucy and Laury," his secretary answered.

Before Weiffenbach could invite them inside, Lucy Schell burst into his office, her husband in tow. Weiffenbach knew them by reputation. Lucy was too big a personality in the Paris automotive scene to go unnoticed.

"You may have heard of us: I am Lucy O'Reilly Schell, and this is my husband Laury." She did not wait for a reply. "We like the look of your new Super-Luxe and want it for the Rally next season. The 138 is too big, so it will have to be a 134."

Laury smiled sheepishly. He was used to Lucy driving the conversation.

Lucy continued, explaining that while the 134 would do for now, her husband thought that Delahaye should put the larger engine of the 138 into the shorter, lighter chassis of the Type 134 to improve its potential as a sports or rally car.

Weiffenbach hesitated for a moment, not least because he was bowled over by the sheer force of personality that had come into his office. Laury had not yet managed a single word.

"What I can do is to prepare a 134 Super-Luxe rally car for you," he said. "It may be rather expensive."

"I'll pay whatever's necessary," Lucy said. They struck a handshake deal.

The car that Lucy was so keen to buy was the fruit of a dramatic change in direction for the Delahaye company, an effort to guarantee its survival. Only a few years before, the French auto industry had boasted over 350 manufacturers; now they were down to a few dozen. The Great Depression and collapse of the export market had decimated their ranks, and even the Big Three—Peugeot, Renault, and Citroën—were on the ropes.

The stolid, reliably conservative Delahaye company, known for building vehicles of consistent quality, had been in dire straits, its production numbers for cars and trucks a fraction of what they had been. Something had to be done or Weiffenbach would have to institute job cuts.

At an extraordinary meeting of the board, it was decided—particularly by senior shareholder Marguerite Desmarais—to raise Delahaye's profile by competing in motor racing and breaking speed records. Few believed Weiffenbach would take such a risk, and fewer still that Delahaye would emerge, as one critic remarked, "into the sunlight from the shadows of a 30-year hibernation." But Monsieur Charles, as Weiffenbach was generally known, was willing to take the gamble if it meant saving the company.

A sturdy and reliable truck from the French manufacturer Delahaye.

Soon after the board meeting, he charged the company's chief designer, Jean François, to lead Delahaye into a new era of fast and agile cars. François was not given free rein to spend whatever he wanted, nor was he given unlimited time. Weiffenbach, as was typical for him, expected François to produce a practical and economic solution, and fast.

In early 1933, he produced not one but two cars, of the same general design: The first, the Type 134, featured a four-cylinder, 2.1-liter engine and independent front suspension on a chassis with a short wheelbase of 112 inches.** The second, more

** Wheelbase is the distance between the front and rear axles.

powerful Type 138 had a six-cylinder, 3.2-liter engine, with the same suspension as the 134 but with a wheelbase a foot longer.

Both engines were based on one that Delahaye had first produced in 1928 for three-ton trucks. Tough, strong, and able to run for long periods at full throttle, the Type 103 truck engine could be forced in a way few car engines could handle. Coupled with independent front suspension, the purpose of which was to keep the tail (wheels, tires, brakes, and assemblies) from unnecessarily wagging the dog (pretty much everything else on the car), the cars handled the road deftly, no matter its surface.

When the two cars were demonstrated as part of the 1933 Paris Motor Show, their performances were a smashing success for Delahaye. Weiffenbach introduced their new design direction, sheathed in sleek bodies and triangular front grilles created by a high-end French carrossier. Like many auto manufacturers, Delahaye produced everything but the bodies of their cars, leaving customers to order bespoke ones from the coachbuilder of their choice.

It did not take long for buyers to appear, and Lucy Schell was one of the first to be captivated by the Delahaye presentation. She wasted little time showing up at the rue du Banquier factory.

PART II

RISE AND FALL

CHAPTER 8

René followed his win at the 1930 Monaco Grand Prix with a victory at the Grand Prix de la Marne at Reims, then, sure of his prospects, he traveled to Molsheim in northern France to ask Ettore Bugatti, head of the firm, for a place on Bugatti's factory team. Embittered over his team's defeat at Monaco, "Le Patron" refused to see him, even though René had achieved his win driving one of the company's cars. The snub struck René almost physically.

He returned heartbroken to Nice, where a note awaited him from Alfieri Maserati, one of the six Maserati brothers involved in the young Italian automobile firm. They wanted to meet with René. Maserati had enjoyed a tremendous season in 1930. Their race cars were fast and sleek but unwieldy to pilot, and one contemporary said that their overly flexible chassis "jumped about on its own suspension like a cat on hot bricks."

At their ramshackle factory in Bologna, a lone secretary was pecking away at her typewriter in a closet-size office. She waved René in to meet the brothers, who wore the same blue overalls as their workers. The Maseratis gave René a tour, then they ate lunch together—a delicious chicken stew—at their favorite restaurant, Il Pappagallo. René signed on to be their lead driver for

1931, the shimmering dream of his youth realized at last. Now he was truly a professional Grand Prix driver.

In 1932, the Grand Prix was essentially *formule libre*: There were no restrictions on engine size, weight, or fuel consumption. The aim was to increase the vehicles' speed, but no thought was given to the cars' handling or safety. Always a high-risk sport, motor racing had become lethally dangerous.

The afternoon of May 22, 1932, was a sultry one at the AVUS track in Berlin. René took off from the start in his lipstick-red Maserati, a sixteen-cylinder, supercharged 5-liter engine that thundered like an aircraft barreling down a runway. It was the fastest car he had ever driven, and he led the race after the first lap of the twelve-mile track. Close behind was Rudi Caracciola, in a 2.3-liter Alfa Romeo, and Manfred von Brauchitsch, in his Mercedes SSKL. Georg Christian Lobkowicz, a well-to-do amateur from Czechoslovakia, was driving a white-and-blue Bugatti T54—a car that was notoriously difficult to pilot.

At the first turn, before the south loop, Lobkowicz found himself sandwiched between two racers. He gave way, but when he tried to avoid a clip of the grass to his right, he swung his wheel a fraction too sharply to the left. At 125 mph, the Bugatti sheared sideways, barreled across the grass strip separating the straights, then leaped up, tumbling and flipping over the course of some sixty feet until it struck a tree and settled in a mangled wreck on a railway embankment. Lobkowicz's skull was fractured in the crash, and he never regained consciousness.

The race continued unabated. Early on, René set a new lap record at 130.5 mph, but then his accelerator began to stick, keeping his speed up even when he wanted to slow down. He managed to release it and headed straight for the pits. "It's over," he said breathlessly to his team as he pulled up.

"No," Ernesto Maserati said. "You must finish the race for your lap record to count." They inspected the car, and Ernesto identified the problem, then tore off a piece of metal from the signal board and jammed it somewhere in the crevices of the Maserati's floorboard.

"It won't work," René said.

"Just finish the race," Ernesto pleaded. "If the accelerator gives you problems, there's always that button on the dash to stop the engine."

René returned to the track, his mind churning over what he would do if the accelerator stuck while he flashed toward the north or south loop. Change gears, hit the brakes, and punch that kill button.

The long pit stop and the accelerator trouble put René in dead last, where he stayed throughout the rest of the race, but he finished—alive. Later, at the hotel, he went to see Ernesto. In his first race with Maserati, the 1931 Tunis Grand Prix, René had suffered a terrible crash that had accordioned his car. A feeling had spawned then that a dark cloud was following him. He had managed to race well enough in his initial season to be invited back and had agreed, mainly because he simply liked the Maserati brothers. They involved him in everything. "What do you think about this?" "Let's discuss that" was their operating style. All the brothers were mechanics themselves, and they were hardworking, honest, and serious. At the end of each day, they dined together, and René felt part of a tight-knit family.

His bad luck refused to lift in his second season. Already that year, he had suffered repeated engine problems, had slammed into a house at the Monaco Grand Prix because of faulty brakes, and now a faulty accelerator had almost got him killed. He wanted off the team, confident now in his ability that he would easily find a new home.

"Please release me," he pleaded. Ernesto agreed.

Later that summer, back driving as an independent, René was heading for his first win of the season. Speeding around the fifteenth, and penultimate, lap of the Grand Prix du Comminges on August 14, 1932, he widened his forty-second lead over his nearest competitor, Jean-Pierre Wimille.

Then, in a sudden shower, rain poured from an overhanging cloud and pelted the spectators in the hillside grandstand overlooking the Pyrenees. The cloud disappeared as quickly as it came, but the road was soaked.

Miles away, zooming along beside the river Garonne in his Bugatti T51, René never even knew about the cloudburst. Minutes later, he shot down the long straight before the uphill curve by the grandstand. As he went into the slick bend at 100 mph, he felt his Bugatti lurch sideways.

The spectators gasped. René twisted the wheel and changed

gears, trying to regain control, all the while fully aware of the horror of what was happening. For a millisecond, he thought he had regained a purchase on the road, when his left rear wheel struck a bump. The slight leap of his tire was enough for the physics of flight to take effect.

The Bugatti soared upward on its front end and corkscrewed in the air. Thrown from the cockpit, René bounced across the pavement like a rock skipped across a pond. His car leveled a tree on the roadside and staggered to a halt in front of the press stand. Dazed, he tried to stand. Officials rushed to his side before he fell, his face covered with blood.

An ambulance hurried him to the local hospital, and as he drifted in and out of consciousness, the doctors cut off his overalls and examined him. He had suffered several bad lacerations and a severe concussion, but no broken bones. For the next week, he stayed in the hospital, reliving the terrifying crash. He had never come closer to dying in a race.

The risk of sudden death had always been intertwined with the allure of motorsport, but never more so than now. Race cars reached average speeds of over 120 mph on several courses. Death's presence, René once said, "hovered around us." Every driver knew that death might carry any one of them away at any time, whether because of faulty brakes, debris on the track, or a fellow competitor's actions. They could not perform if fear was a factor, and so they looked at death with something more like respect.

René loved his life as a race-car driver. The tinkering with

René Dreyfus crash... Prix, 1932.

engines, the travel, the competition, the fame. He was young and flush with cash, getting newspaper headlines and attention everywhere he went. Even better, the other drivers felt like his family. They traveled together from race to race in flashy cabriolets. They stayed at the same lavish hotels. They dined and drank at the same white-cloth restaurants and tony bars. After races, there was usually a tuxedoed gala where they partied together, away from the autograph hunters. During the winter, they skied together in the Alps. Their girlfriends and wives were often friends with one another. It was a strange kind of friendship. The racers could enjoy a laugh together one night and the next afternoon exhaust every effort to beat each other on the track, even if that meant almost running each other off it.

René loved driving above all else, that feeling of being behind the wheel in balance with the machine. All he wanted was to get back to the track, even though the dangers were now very real to him in ways they had not been when he was a young kid flinging his first Bugatti around the hills outside Nice.

After leaving the hospital, René entered a couple more races, but he retired from both. He had done well as an independent that season and finished the year ranked the fifth-best Grand Prix driver. In the right car, with the right team, he might even realize his ambition to be European Champion.

That fall, he was invited to lunch by Bartolomeo "Meo" Costantini. A flying ace in World War I, Meo Costantini had competed in Bugattis after the war, winning several major races, before becoming the team manager for the firm. Over lunch, the tall, stately, and often solemn Costantini made his offer for René to join Bugatti.

"I'm ready," René said mildly—though he wanted to leap with joy from his chair.

The following day, he signed the contract and met Ettore Bugatti. Sporting his trademark brown bowler hat, Le Patron was in his early fifties, with a round, fleshy face, blue eyes, and hands that were in almost constant motion, like an orchestra conductor's. The two men shook on their agreement, René beaming with delight.

CHAPTER 9

Accompanied by the stirring classical music of German com-
poser Richard Wagner, Adolf Hitler strode into the Hall of
Honor on Berlin's Kaiserdamm. Just twelve days before, on
January 30, 1933, he had been named chancellor of Germany,
an occasion marked by a torchlight parade led by a tide of his
brownshirted, jackbooted supporters. The new chancellor
planned to deliver one of his first major speeches at that year's
Berlin Motor Show.

His voice quaked with a passion that was amplified by loudspeakers as he declared his intention to slash the taxes and
regulations that were suppressing the motor industry, to build a
nationwide highway system, and to dominate international
motorsport. Also present at the motor show that year was
Korpsführer Adolf Hühnlein, whom Hitler had personally put
in command of the National Socialist Motor Corps (NSKK).
The purpose of the NSKK was to train a legion of men in motor
skills, establishing the foundation of a mechanized army.

Hitler's promises significantly brightened prospects for sales
at Daimler-Benz. Over the past decade, as the Nazi leader came
closer and closer to power, the automobile company had drawn
itself closer and closer to him. Jakob Werlin, head of their Munich
dealership, had long built a friendship with Hitler. Even before

Hitler and his "cavalry of the future," including (first row, left to right) Bernd Rosemeyer, Rudi Caracciola, Adolf Hitler, Hans Stuck, Adolf Hühnlein (in uniform), and Ernst Henne; (second row far left) Manfred von Brauchitsch.

the failed Putsch in 1923, Werlin had sold Hitler his first Mercedes, and he continued to provide discounted vehicles for Hitler's cross-country political campaigns. Over the next ten years, he became a self-declared "personal confidant" of Hitler, as well as a member of the Schutzstaffel (SS), the Nazis' fearsome paramilitary force.

When the Daimler-Benz board gathered in the Stuttgart head-quarters in March 1933, CEO Wilhelm Kissel focused on how to continue to build on this close relationship. Daimler-Benz already advertised in the Nazi party's newspapers. It gained favor with Hitler by sending its most successful and famous drivers to visit him. Board members raised funds for the Nazis and solicited the party's top officials to engage the firm in the event of the rearmament of the military. Using Jakob Werlin as a go-between, Kissel ensured that Hitler was aware that "he will be able to rely on us in the future, as in the past."

Now that Hitler had ascended to the position of chancellor, Daimler-Benz needed him far more than he needed them. With car and truck sales plummeting by half from their record high in 1928, Kissel believed that government support was the best path out of the crisis.

Orders for heavy trucks were on the rise, and there was a clear signal that Hitler intended to restore the German military in direct violation of the Versailles Treaty that had ended World War I. Prototypes for airplane engines and tanks had already been ordered. If they moved toward full-scale production, it would be a huge boon to filling the excess capacity at many of their plants.

A return to racing would be a crucial next step: Wins on the international stage would provide a publicity bonanza, particularly for the export market. However, Kissel knew that engineering race cars for the new 1934 formula—and financing a team of drivers and staff—would be expensive. His staff calculated that the company would need to spend at least 1 million marks a year to reign supreme in the Grand Prix (7.5 million in today's US dollars). Only through state funding could this ambition be realized. Therein lay the problem.

Auto Union, the result of a merger between four Depression-hobbled German manufacturers (Horch, Audi, DKW, and Wanderer), was also asking for state sponsorship of its racing program. They had already contracted Ferdinand Porsche to design a car under the new formula. The brilliant engineer had launched his own charm offensive on Hitler, complimenting him in a letter after the motor show for his "profound speech" and his desire to "place our skill and determination at the disposal of the German people."

Kissel presented his company's board with the draft of a letter suggesting to the "Highly Esteemed Herr Reich Chancellor" that state funding was needed to compete aggressively in the Grand Prix and that Daimler-Benz alone should receive it. The letter concluded, "Since in the course of the company's history . . . our marque has contributed frequently and significantly to the respect paid to Germany at sporting events, we would dedicate all our skill and knowledge to this and would deem it an honor if we were enabled to represent the German flag in the sport of the future."

They soon received their answer. The Reich would fund 1 million marks . . . but the sum would be split between Daimler-Benz and Auto Union, and Korpsführer Hühnlein would oversee all their efforts in the Grand Prix. Although they received only half of what they thought they needed to support a team, Kissel and his board knew they had no choice but to accept—and to do their best to bring a winning race car to the new formula.

Recruitment for drivers began. Manfred von Brauchitsch was

eager. Negotiations were ongoing with veteran Mercedes driver Hans Stuck (who eventually decided to race for Auto Union). The big question was Rudi Caracciola. He was committed to his own team for 1933, but Alfred Neubauer had secured a promise that he would give Mercedes first refusal the following year.

Rudi Caracciola blazed around the streets of Monaco in a 2.3-liter Alfa Romeo, painted white with a blue stripe down its side. A short distance behind followed Louis Chiron, also in an Alfa—his blue with a white stripe. The colors were a nod to their French-German partnership.

The previous fall, Rudi and Charly Caracciola had hosted Louis and his long-time girlfriend, Alice Hoffmann, at their chalet in the Swiss Alps. Despite having had successful seasons, both men had been let go from their teams—Louis because of personal conflict with Bugatti, and Rudi because Alfa Romeo had decided to abandon its works team, much in the same way Mercedes had the year before.

"You know," said Chiron, "Why should we always win the prizes for other people? It would be much smarter to start our own firm." Thus, Scuderia CC, after their two initials, was born.

The two drivers shot past the Monaco pits, on their twenty-fourth practice lap. In a Grand Prix first, the starting grid on the day of the race would be determined by the best times achieved during three days of practice. On the initial day, Rudi and Louis focused more on testing out their Alfa Romeos than anything else. Louis had never driven the make before, but under a sky

Rudi Caracciola and Louis Chiron, partners in Scuderia CC.

pocked with black clouds, the two drivers managed to clock the fastest laps that morning.

On their last run of the morning on Thursday, April 20, 1933, Rudi continued to lead down the corkscrew turns to the seafront with Louis on his tail. Rudi zipped through the chicane, then accelerated down the straight toward the left-hand turn at Tabac Corner. A glance in his mirror showed Louis nowhere in sight.

He braked slightly while looking in his rearview mirror to see where his teammate had gone. Suddenly, his Alfa went into a skid. Only one of the front brakes had engaged, he thought, as the car swept at 70 mph toward the low stone parapet that separated the promenade from the sea.

Time slowed to a crawl.

Rudi cranked down through the gears. Calculating that he was more likely to survive a smash into Tabac Corner than a leap into the water, he steered away from the parapet. Hands tight on the wheel, he tried to regain control. The car snaked left, then right. At last he regained control, but it was too late. The Alfa struck the wall first by the right wheel, then the whole side panel. The body of the car crumpled against the stone. Then the car propelled sideways for a few dozen feet before coming to a juddering stop.

Rudi wanted only to be free of the car that seemed to have molded itself around his body. With strength born of shock, he wrested himself out of his seat. People were dashing down the steps from the upper road toward him. There was no need, Rudi thought: He was fine. *No trouble here other than a wrecked car.*

Behind him he heard a squealing stop and saw Louis Chiron jump out of his car. Rudi tried to take a step forward . . . and an explosion of pain overwhelmed him. His right leg gave out, and only Louis's arrival at his side prevented him from collapsing onto the road. He was carried away from the track in a simple wooden chair taken from a café.

At last an ambulance arrived, and its crew jostled him inside. Each bump and turn through the streets of Monte Carlo sent ripples of pain down his leg. Something was very wrong with it. He dared not ask what. At the hospital, he was carted first into the X-ray lab, then into the surgery ward.

Waiting for the doctor, he stared through the high windows at the treetops waving in the wind. The pain he had felt earlier was only a fraction of the agony that swallowed him now. His face was cut in several places, and the grim lock of his jaw spoke of his suffering. The results of the X-ray were appalling. The femur and the entire tibia were completely smashed. He was not expected to ever be able to drive again.

Three days later, he lay in his hospital bed, listening to the Grand Prix on the radio. Charly sat beside him, and flowers from well-wishers covered every available surface. In the final lap, near the finish, the engine of Tazio Nuvolari's Alfa Romeo caught on fire. He leaped out and tried to push the car to the finish line, enveloped in billowing black smoke. Achille Varzi, driving a Bugatti, won easily, followed by Mario Borzacchini, with René Dreyfus in third. Louis Chiron was a distant fourth.

Rudi was stunned that he had not recovered in time. He *belonged* in that race. But the evidence was there in the bulky plaster cast that encased his right leg up to the hip. Only a hurried consultation with a specialist had saved it from the saw. His legs would never be a balanced pair again, and he would have a permanent limp.

He felt he had lost his place in the world.

CHAPTER 10

After the Grand Prix, René Dreyfus and his Bugatti teammates dined on lobster at the Monte Carlo Casino and celebrated their pooled winnings. A reporter interrupted their party to ask some questions about the race, but they said nothing about Rudi Caracciola.

It was awful to see one of their fellow drivers crash and get so badly injured, but dwelling on such calamities only increased the chance that they might suffer doubts that would affect their performance on the track. Death was something they understood intimately. They had seen it so often, had come so close to it so many times. They measured how fast to take a corner by how likely it was they would kill themselves in the act of doing so.

René followed his third-place finish at Monaco with the same position at the Belgian Grand Prix and with two second places at the Dieppe and Nice Grands Prix. First place eluded him, chiefly because Bugattis were simply behind the times when compared to the Alfa Romeos and Maseratis.

It was while he was based in Molsheim and driving for Bugatti that René fell in love. Nicknamed "Chou-Chou" (in French, the equivalent of "Sweetie"), Gilberte Miraton was one of a string of wealthy young women who frequented the racetracks and modeled the latest fashions while competing in Concours d'Élégance events—Chou-Chou with her grand white Delage.

Chou-Chou and René crossed paths in early 1933. Vivacious, funny, and whip-smart, she was impossible to overlook. She was short and dark-haired and had the kind of presence that drew the attention of everyone in the room. Whenever possible, René visited her at her home in Châtel-Guyon, a spa town near Vichy in central France, or they met at races. As his first season with Bugatti neared an end, René was happy and content.

In mid-November, Alfred Neubauer paid Rudi Caracciola a visit in Lugano, Switzerland, where he and Charly were living while he rehabilitated after his accident. The cartilage in his right leg had not healed properly, and his right leg was now two inches shorter than his left. Rudi's surgeon had advised that walking was likely ambition enough. When Rudi heard that, he felt a coldness spread inside his body.

Between periods of rest on the terrace overlooking the lake, Rudi tried to spend more and more time on his feet. Despite using crutches, each swing of his leg sent a shot of pain through his hip.

Rudi greeted the Mercedes team manager, who gave him a great hug, then they went out to sit on the terrace. Rudi sensed his every move—and facial expression—was under inspection. He had hidden the plaster cast, which he was still obliged to wear, under loose trousers.

As always, Neubauer got straight to the point. Hitler was

supporting Daimler-Benz in developing a new race car for the 1934 season. Manfred von Brauchitsch and Italian champion Luigi Fagioli had already signed onto the team. They needed him. Neubauer wanted to know if Rudi could drive again.

"Of course, I can," Rudi said, before brazenly asking about the contract. Neubauer waved

Alfred Neubauer and his protégé Rudi Caracciola.

away the question. Rudi needed to come to Stuttgart to discuss that—perhaps in January.

After Neubauer returned to Germany, Rudi learned through a friend that the team manager had reported to Kissel that there was little chance Rudi would compete ever again. They had written him off and were looking for younger, fitter drivers.

The plaster cast came off at last in December, and every day, Rudi tried to walk a little farther, his cane in one hand, Charly holding the other. He was gathering strength, but his uneven legs made for an awkward gait, and the pain in his hip never faded.

In early January 1934, he and Charly traveled to Stuttgart. Rudi had pushed for a meeting with the Daimler-Benz CEO so he could tell him he was fit enough to drive. Kissel was unconvinced but promised that Neubauer would sit down with him later that evening to discuss it.

Neubauer came directly to Rudi's room at the Graf Zeppelin Hotel. As he had done with Kissel, Rudi masked his limp and gritted his teeth through the strain. "Fit and well again?" Neubauer asked. Rudi swore that he was. Neubauer reminded him of the strength needed to brake and accelerate hundreds of times during a race. "What guarantee is there that you won't crack up in the middle?"

It was at that point that Charly lost her temper, suggesting that their precious new car might "crack up" first.

At last, Neubauer offered Rudi a compromise. In May, when the car was ready for testing, Rudi could participate in a practice run. If he passed muster, he would be on the team.

The following day, Neubauer brought Rudi to the Mercedes plant in Untertürkheim, just outside Stuttgart, to show him the new car. They passed a series of huge workshops to arrive at a small building surrounded by a high, barbed-wire fence. A guard checked their identification before allowing them through the gate. Everything about their work was top secret, Neubauer warned. Inside the workshop, Rudi got his first look at the engine and the overall design of Mercedes's latest Grand Prix car: the W25.

The theory behind the 1934 formula was straightforward: If factory teams wanted more powerful engines, the chassis and everything else needed to be heavier to hold the engines to the road; with weight limited to 750 kg (1,650 pounds), speed would therefore also be limited. Dr. Hans Nibel, head of Mercedes's design department, figured differently. In his interpretation, the formula allowed an *unlimited* engine size if they could design a lightweight chassis and running gear that had the ability to corner, brake, steer, and hold to the road while traveling at very high speeds.

Achieving such driving performance was no small matter. The prototype Mercedes engine, a supercharged 3.3-liter straight-eight,** which Rudi saw mounted on a dynamometer, was an absolute thoroughbred. Although not a revolutionary design, it benefited from ultraprecise construction and a host of improvements. As the dynamometer showed, the engine produced horsepower measurements 50 percent greater than the Alfa P3. Nibel matched the engine with a platform built of light alloys wherever possible.

The W25 was a single-seater—new territory for Mercedes-Benz. It featured front- and rear-wheel independent suspension as well as better weight distribution. All in all, the W25 promised to ride balanced and tight to the ground. If everything was tuned correctly, it would be the fastest race car ever to grace the Grand Prix.

Having seen what was in store for the team's drivers, Rudi was more motivated than ever before to return to competition. Back home, he went out for walks with Charly, venturing farther and farther each time. He accepted that he would never again move without pain. The real question was his ability to endure a 500-mile race in the tight cockpit of the W25.

** A straight-eight is an engine in which all eight cylinders are mounted in a straight line.

On February 2, Charly headed off for a day's skiing with some friends. She was reluctant to go, but Rudi convinced her that she deserved at least a day off after ten months of nursing him.

Later that afternoon, he hobbled down the hill to meet her at the train station. Neither she nor any of her ski companions showed up at the appointed hour. He returned home.

The sun set, and still there was no sign of Charly. Rudi sat in the chalet, lights out, so he could see her coming up the road. At 10 p.m., the guide who had led her tour approached the door. One look at him and Rudi went white.

Words followed: There had been an avalanche . . . Charly was dead. Without her, and without his racing, there was nothing left in his life.

CHAPTER 11

At the Delahaye factory, hammers pealed, machine tools grumbled, compressed air hissed. The smell of ground metal, oil, grease, lacquer, and the heavy effort of a team of workers permeated the air. Past them strode Lucy Schell, once again headed toward the office of Charles Weiffenbach.

She was incensed. Not only had his company missed the delivery date of her Delahaye Type 134, preventing her from competing in the Monte Carlo Rally in January 1934, but he had then supplied the very model she'd proposed to his factory driver, Albert Perrot, to participate in the rally himself. Perrot placed a dismal twenty-fourth out of 114 participants.

It was an experiment only, Monsieur Charles said, trying to pacify her. Then he further stoked her anger by revealing that he was supplying a pair of that same "experiment," 138 Specials, to two of her rivals in the all-female Saint-Raphaël Rally, Mademoiselle Gonnot and Madame Nenot. The two women were longtime Delahaye customers, Monsieur Charles said. Surely, she must understand.

Lucy did not, and later, to prove her point, she crushed two 138 Specials in the Saint-Raphaël Rally, driving her rather less powerful Delahaye 134 to a fourth place overall. After the event, she visited the Delahaye factory again. This time she was unequivocal. She wanted a 138 Special of her own for the Paris–Nice Rally so she could prove herself to be the "best Delahaye rally driver in the land"—man or woman.

Weiffenbach agreed, not least because he wanted to use any of Lucy's wins to advertise his new line of cars. There was something else: He liked Lucy Schell. She was every bit as pertinacious, combative, and perservering as he considered himself to be.

In motorsport, Lucy was up against a male-dominated world, one that was riddled with sexism from its earliest days. Organizers spent an inordinate amount of time thinking about what female drivers should wear (lest, ridiculously, their skirts blow up over their heads) rather than about how well they were competing. According to *La Vie Automobile*, women were "weak and delicate by definition" and therefore ill suited to the "muscular efforts" needed to start a car, change the tires, brake, or steer. Another editorialist claimed that women cared little about an automobile's power or handling abilities; they were "only attentive to the aesthetic factor." Speed queens like Elisabeth Junek, who was a specialist of the Targa Florio, the Sicilian open-road endurance race that was considered one of the toughest in the world, revealed these claims to be ridiculous. But many organizers continued to forbid the couple dozen competitive female drivers from their races outright. Others allowed them only as co-drivers. They were a rarity in Grand Prix events, and factory teams refused to let them join their ranks.

As for their fellow male race-car drivers, they seldom gave the

The prototype Delahaye world-record breaker that inspired the 138 Special

women the credit they deserved. One driver joked, "They chase after us on the track; we chase after them off it." When passing female drivers in a race, Louis Chiron liked to blow them kisses. To buck the prejudice she encountered in every room she entered, and in every competition she signed up for, Lucy had to be supremely competent and forceful in what she wanted.

Insulated by her fortune, Lucy was able to focus on racing, but she worried constantly about France and its strength among nations. Although neither wholly French nor American, she had spent much of her adult life living in and around Paris. She had served there in World War I. Her sons had been born there. She believed that France must find its footing against an emboldened Fascist Germany, but it was beyond even her sturdy self-belief to think that she could have a role. Her energies were instead bent toward competing on an equal level with the men who dominated the sport she loved.

On Saturday, March 24, Lucy arrived for the start of the Paris–Nice Rally. She and her five fellow speed queens (out of a total field of forty) posed arm in arm in front of their cars for photographers. Chapeau tilted on the side of her head, black fitted jacket zipped to her throat, and wearing heels, Lucy looked like she had just stepped off the Champs-Élysées after shopping for the latest spring fashions. She then changed into her racing overalls.

The Paris–Nice Rally was more like a decathlon—a series of events—when compared to the grueling marathon that was the Monte Carlo Rally. First run in 1922, it served to spotlight the speed, stamina, flexibility, braking, road handling, and acceleration abilities of the entrant cars—and their drivers' ability to show them at their best.

In her new Delahaye 138 Special, Lucy set off through a morning fog on the first stage. Half an hour later, the sky cleared, and she kept a steady pace south toward Marseille, 750 kilometers (466 miles) away. There were some spells of rain en route, but she finished well within the allotted time as dusk settled over the southern port city.

The next day, she ranked third-best in the kilometer acceleration test up the hill of Marseille's Boulevard Michelet. On Monday, she ran the 200 kilometers (125 miles) to Nice, again right on schedule. In the afternoon, and the next day, she was eighth in the 500-meter (545 yards) flying-start contest and performed well in the braking and steering tests.

For the final stage of the Paris–Nice Rally, the La Turbie hill climb, Lucy barreled away from the start, uncowed by the first sharp turn, with its etched stone marking the spot where, on April 1, 1903, Count Eliot Zborowski snagged his cuff link on the hand throttle and, unable to slow, failed to make the turn. His Mercedes had slammed into the wall.

After the turn that claimed Zborowski, Lucy sped up one of the steepest sections of the course. Bordered by sunflower-colored villas and palm trees, the road headed north, away from the coast, in a series of soft S-bends and long straights that allowed her to push the 138 Special almost to its maximum. The climb steepened again as she headed east toward the finish across

from Èze, a town perched like an eagle's nest on a peak between the Grand Corniche and the coastline. She finished the course with the tenth-best time of 5 minutes 26.6 seconds and was eighth in the overall ranking, first in her engine class, and first again among the female drivers.

At the Automobile Club de Nice the following night, when the race's organizers celebrated the winners, her "admirable virtuosity" as a driver was lauded equally with her "perfect" Delahaye 138 Special.

CHAPTER 12

After Charly's funeral, Rudi holed himself up in his Swiss chalet, surrounded by the trinkets of his former victories. He went out only after dusk so nobody would see him stumbling forward on his cane.

In early April, having almost withered away in this self-made prison, he agreed to drive the lap of honor at Monte Carlo, the new formula's inaugural competition. To the applause of thousands, he drove a Mercedes convertible around the course. At the halfway point, the pain in his right leg forced him to switch to using his left foot to brake and accelerate.

When he returned to the harbor, the starting grid was assembled, the engines were revving. There were Chiron, Nuvolari, Varzi, Dreyfus . . . Rudi ached to be among them. He left before the second lap was finished. "For me, there had to be a comeback . . . Otherwise life was pointless," he wrote when he returned to Arosa. As a race-car driver, "you are the will that controls this creature of steel; you think for it, you are in tune with its rhythm. And your brain works with the same speed and precision as this heart of steel. Or else the monster turns master over you and destroys you. I had to drive. There was nothing else for me."

While the motorsport world carried on without him, Rudi

continued to strengthen his leg with daily bouts of physical therapy in preparation for his trial run in the W25.

He arrived at AVUS at 6 a.m. on May 24, having asked for a dawn start in order to avoid the press. This was his first time behind the wheel of a race car in over a year, and he feared he might falter.

The single-seater car, now sheathed in a sleek white-painted aluminum body with a short tail and a headrest that tapered away from the driver, looked fast and nimble. Rudi pulled up beside it in his convertible, saving himself a tiring—and potentially embarrassing—walk from the pits. He looked every inch his former race-car driver self, in white overalls and his old leather racing shoes, a scarf tied close around his neck. All that was different was the walking cane.

He could sense Neubauer and his crew inspecting his every move, no doubt eager to know if their premier driver's star had dimmed for good. A pair of mechanics helped him into the small cockpit, causing his leg to start hurting already. The seat had been sized to fit his body from old measurements, but the crew had adjusted the placement of the accelerator and the brake to compensate for his now shorter right leg. As Rudi gripped the steering wheel, a company photographer snapped him in profile before being shooed away.

Rudi lowered his goggles and signaled for the mechanics to start the engine. Its reverberations caused his heart to beat faster. He shifted into first gear and eased down the track where he had claimed his first Grand Prix victory. He wanted to raise his fist in triumph: He was driving again.

With each lap, he increased speed, the supercharger screaming at a higher and higher pitch. By the fourth lap, he was traveling so fast that the trees beside the track blurred. The car was extremely quick—and very powerful.

One Mercedes driver likened it to handling a fast touring car on ice. Too much gas, too heavy a touch on the steering wheel, and it would spin around on its rear wheels or launch off the road without an instant's notice. Such was his skill that Rudi was able to handle it on his first run.

After the eighth lap, Neubauer flagged him into the pits. Reassured by Rudi's driving, he invited him to join the Mercedes team. One of the requirements of doing so was that he would also have to join the NSKK, which, Rudi knew, was a paramilitary branch of the Nazi party akin to the SA and the SS.

He did not hesitate.

The Germans' silver-bodied race cars competed outside their own country for the first time at the French Grand Prix in 1934. On July 1, in scorching temperatures, 80,000 spectators made the journey to Montlhéry, site of a giant concrete autodrome and notoriously tough road circuit set on a hilltop fifteen miles from Paris. Loudspeakers announced the arrival of the racers, and René Dreyfus, in his Bugatti Type 59, was among those who advanced onto the track. The cars from Mercedes and Auto Union followed, their bodies draped with swastika flags.

Rumors were circulating about the new Mercedes car. *Motor Sport* reported secondhand accounts of its remarkable speed during winter tests at the Monza track. According to spectators, "the tearing exhaust note is even more stirring than the howl of the blower gears in the famous SSKs." As René later wrote, it was clear that the German chancellor intended "his country's cars to be supreme, the most powerful, the fastest, the most everything."

He could not say the same of Ettore Bugatti. The two-seater Type 59 was a low-slung beauty with piano-wire wheels and the classic horseshoe-shaped front, but it was difficult to handle on the road, and it often jumped out of gear. When René mentioned this, Bugatti simply told him, "Well, that's too bad. You'll have to get used to it."

During practice, René witnessed the utter superiority of the German cars. They were quicker off the line, faster down the straights, and with their all-independent wheel suspension, they stuck tight to the road during sharp turns at speeds few had ever witnessed. With their drivers seated so far forward, the Auto Union cars looked particularly revolutionary, but both German designs were streamlined in a way that proclaimed a sudden leap into the future.

Their shiny aluminum bodies, a departure from the typical German white, accentuated the impression and soon earned the sobriquet "the Silver Arrows." Next to them, on the starting grid at Montlhéry, René's Bugatti resembled an antique.

At last the engines cranked into life. The drivers could barely think over what one reporter called the "banshee wail" of the Mercedes superchargers—"the noisiest car on earth," according

The new W25 Mercedes Silver Arrow.

to *Autocar*. After the starting flag fell, the multicolored band of cars howled down the low-walled straight and through the narrow opening that led from the autodrome to the road circuit.

Rudi was in first position by the westernmost bend of the 12.5-kilometer (7.76-mile) course. The wheels of his Mercedes and those of the Auto Union cars clung smoothly to the sharp turns while their competitors seemed to bump and leap across the pavement. Nevertheless, by the time they returned to the oval bowl, Chiron was in the lead in his scarlet Alfa P3. Despite driving for Scuderia Ferrari, an Italian team, he was greeted with a roar of appreciation from the mostly French crowd in the stands. His teammate, Achille Varzi, was close behind, then Rudi. René was eighth.

One car after another cracked up from the extraordinary average speeds of over 90 mph. First to fail was an Auto Union P-Wagen, after an hour, then Brauchitsch's W25, then a Maserati. On the fourteenth lap, Luigi Fagioli's Mercedes limped into the pits and died. Two laps later, Rudi was forced to abandon his at the far end of the course.

The Mercedes team was now out of the race altogether, and the German radio commentator went silent. "The mighty German assault," Chiron later described, "was simply melting away in the summer sunshine."

In the seventeenth lap, René's engine began misfiring. A long pit stop appeared to solve the issue—fouled spark plugs—but then his car died on the next lap. Another teammate fell out soon after.

Hell-bent on winning the forty-lap race, Chiron roared around the course in his P3, throttle wide open, a persistent swirl of dust behind him. Auto Union's Hans Stuck gave him a good chase, his engine's throaty vibrations almost shaking the ground beneath the car as it traveled around the ribbon of road. In lap 32, he also retired because of mechanical issues, taking the last of the Silver Arrows out of the race.

Despite the withdrawal of all the German cars, the race was far from being a failure for them. Anyone who saw the silver squadron maneuver the course at previously impossible speeds understood that once their teething troubles were cured, they might well be unbeatable.

Chiron finished first in record speed, averaging 85 mph over the course. Varzi was second, and another Ferrari driver third—a sweep for the Scuderia Ferrari team and their Alfa Romeo P3s. The home crowd was pleased that Louis had won, but their pleasure was tempered by the fact that he was piloting an Italian car, for an Italian team.

Not a single Bugatti—the only French make in the race—had finished, nor had one even come close to the front while they were on the track. The race was a national embarrassment, spurring demands for something to be done if a French car were ever to win another Grand Prix, particularly against the Silver Arrows.

CHAPTER 13

Two weeks later, under an overcast July sky, 150,000 fans descended on the Nürburgring for the German Grand Prix. The nearest town, Adenau, was too small to house the huge crowds who arrived to witness the new breed of race cars that their Führer had spawned. Many had camped out in the pine-forested hillsides, and a regiment of brownshirts had marched for weeks all the way from Berlin, timing their arrival for the start of the race.

From his position on the starting grid, Rudi Caracciola had a front-row seat to the pageantry. A row of swastika flags flew above the grandstand. Soldiers paraded up and down, and a Stuka plane flew low over the circuit. As its booming roar faded, a brass band strutted out onto the track, followed by the arrival of Korpsführer Hühnlein, "Supreme Chief of Nazi Motorsport," in the back of a Mercedes convertible, his route lined by NSKK motorcycle troops wearing black crash helmets.

Hühnlein was accustomed to pomp and obeisance. A battalion commander in World War I, he left the army in 1920 to join the Nazi party after hearing Hitler speak about Germany "never bending, never capitulating." After the Beer Hall Putsch, where the Nazis attempted to overtake the Bavarian government by violent means, Hühnlein and Hitler had spent six months together in Landsberg prison.

Surrounded by other Nazi high officials, Hühnlein stood as the national anthem played: "Deutschland, Deutschland über alles, / Über alles in der Welt." An enormous swastika flag unfurled over the grandstand. When the anthem was finished, he stepped forward in his medal-bedecked uniform to announce the start of the race. Fifty-two years of age, Hühnlein was short of stature and had a grim, purposeful face, heavy jowls, and a high tuft of blondish-brown hair swept back from his balding round head. One got the impression from his look that he would rather chew stones than smile.

Known to be a frank, roughneck "man of action," he had fulfilled the NSKK's mandate by Nazifying the national automobile clubs, starting driver schools, and recruiting hundreds of thousands of members. He promoted the "battle for the motorization of Germany" tirelessly. Before the start of the 1934 season, he sat down with both Mercedes and Auto Union and charted out their race schedules to maximize German victory.

To remain in Hühnlein's favor, the auto companies bowed to his demands on everything from what races they would run to how much affection their drivers could show their wives or girlfriends on the trackside, to agreeing to promote the NSKK as "the cavalry of the future" at motor shows or political events whenever they were asked to do so. Their drivers' celebrity and star power were perfect propaganda and recruitment tools.

In return, the Nazi government poured money into the company's coffers—907,000 marks to Daimler-Benz alone, 40 percent of its team's budget since its relaunch and almost double the amount promised by Hitler.

After the blast of a military cannon, the race began. Neubauer watched from the pits, his large signal board at the ready. It occured to him just how tough a man Rudi Caracciola was to manage the twenty-five laps of

Adolf Hühnlein, Mercedes driver Hermann Lang, and Joseph Goebbels at a race.

the Nürburgring course with his damaged leg—a torturous 172 bends. But the truth was that Rudi had yet to notch a victory.

Like his fellow Mercedes drivers and NSKK members, Rudi wanted to see Germany return to having the international status it had enjoyed before defeat at the end of World War I, but Rudi wanted to win only for himself, to prove that he was back at the top of the game after his accident. None of the pomp and pageantry mattered to him. Only speed. His W25 was running faster than ever because of a new fuel the mechanics dubbed "WW." Consisting of 86 percent methyl alcohol, 8.8 percent acetone, 4.4 percent nitro-benzol, and 0.8 percent ether, it might just as well have been rocket fuel.

For the first dozen laps, Rudi held tight to the leader, Hans Stuck. In the thirteenth, he passed Stuck in a long turn, setting a new track record. However, Rudi had pushed the W25 too hard, and the pistons were seizing up, forcing him to retire. Stuck claimed the victory for Auto Union. Rudi was disappointed, but the race had proved he'd lost none of his old fire.

Hühnlein cared only that it was a German car that first raced past the checkered flag, allowing him the opportunity to give another lengthy speech about the glory of the Reich before telegramming Hitler the great news.

More victories followed for the Germans. During the Italian Grand Prix at Monza, Stuck again had the lead. After ten laps, Neubauer waved a flag, signaling Rudi to go faster. Already in intense pain, he cooperated nonetheless. Twenty laps. Thirty. Forty. Each time he braked, it felt like someone had jabbed a knife into his thigh. In the fifty-ninth lap, he took first position. Stuck pulled off for a pit stop. Rudi wanted to go on—he could win now—but the strain was too much. There was another fifty-seven laps to go, two more hours of driving.

He pulled into the pits. He could barely mutter the words to ask Luigi Fagioli, whose own car had broken down, to take over. The mechanics needed to lift him out of the car; it was impossible for him to stand. Fagioli finished first, giving Rudi a half share in the win, but it was little comfort. If he couldn't complete a race, he would lose his spot on the team and his only reason to awaken each morning.

CHAPTER 14

Throughout 1934, René suffered a horrible string of performances, managing only one significant victory: the Belgian Grand Prix in late July. Forty-eight hours before the race, the Germans had backed out because Belgian customs demanded huge duties for their 3,000 liters of alcohol-based fuel. He was stuck in third place when the two Alfas in front of him dropped out because of mechanical trouble. Therefore, his success could be attributed to luck alone.

The following week, in Nice, his Bugatti stalled while heading into a turn and he crashed into a wall of straw bales. The French press was hounding him for failing to live up to the early promise he had shown at Monaco in 1930. Some were even calling him "the Old Man," although he was only twenty-nine, because his hair was turning gray.

Journalist Georges Fraichard of *L'Intransigent* accused René of having never been the same since his accident at Comminges and puzzled as to whether this was because of misfortune or a lack of nerve. When René was honest with himself, he had to admit that he was missing some of his previous fire; he was too careful.

At the Swiss Grand Prix, in late August, he was determined to prove that he still deserved to be ranked among the best. Le

Patron had not planned on entering the team in the inaugural Swiss Grand Prix, but René convinced him, and he was the only member of the team to make the journey to Berne.

Every inch of the cobblestoned city seemed to be decked out for the event. Cake-shop windows were filled with race-themed confections, and the official poster, which featured a silver and a red car in an impressionist swoosh before stark blue mountains, could be seen on every wall. Flags from Germany, Italy, England, and France flew from the flagpoles in front of the Bellevue Hotel, a grand nineteenth-century palace with views of the Swiss Alps.

Although everyone was staying in the same hotel, as usual—in this case the Bellevue—René found the other drivers rarely ventured away from their teams to sit down and have a chat with one another. The Germans stayed to themselves. The Italians and French likewise. Practice days were the same. The Silver Arrow cars were cordoned off by rope and draped with thick cloth to avoid prying eyes. Photographers were shooed away whenever an engine hood was opened.

The German teams, especially Mercedes, brought a small army with them to the pits. Every advantage, even a half second in a refuel stop or tire change, was sought in their effort to win—not only for the Reich but also for the government bonuses they would earn with each top finish.

On race day, August 26, Hans Stuck leaped into an early lead. Pushing hard, especially in the corners, René fought his way past Nuvolari and Chiron to take second position, but he could not close on Stuck's P-Wagen. Five laps from the finish, he was forced to pull into the pits due to an overheated engine, and by the time he returned to the track, another Auto Union driver, August Momberger, had passed him. René placed third, but in the confusion over his pit stop, the pro-French, pro-Bugatti part of the crowd thought he was in second. Over the loudspeakers, the announcer stated the correct finishing order.

"No, Dreyfus was second," yelled his fan base. Furious at the perceived slight to Momberger, the pro-German fans went wild. Fights broke out in the grandstands. To quell the violence, the race organizers asked René to come to the microphone to confirm the fact that he had indeed finished third. The whole experience left him depressed. His sport had become lost in the widening chasm between countries. Races were now a battleground between nations rather than individual drivers, and the Nazis were clearly investing to dominate.

After the race, Louis Chiron hinted to René that Enzo Ferrari might like him on his team the following year. A few days later, René sat down with the Bugatti manager, Meo Costantini, to discuss his future. Costantini did not try to convince René to stay. But he had some advice for him. Looking down at his big calloused hands, Costantini spoke in his usual pointed manner: "René, you could be one of the greatest drivers in the world were it not for the one thing: You are not aggressive enough. You are too steady, too dependable."

His early success had come to him easily, Costantini continued, and he urged René to find something to struggle and fight for. Until that time, greatness would elude him. The criticism

Meo Constantini and Ettore Bugatti in the 1920s.

cut deep, but René knew that Constantini was right.

He left Molsheim with the gift of a watch, an offer to join Scuderia Ferrari, and an announcement in the social pages that he and Chou-Chou were engaged to be married.

Two weeks before their December 8 wedding, they traveled to Châtel-Guyon to spend time with her family. Chou-Chou and her father had two matters they wanted to discuss with René. First, Monsieur Miraton proposed that René consider retiring from motorsport to join his pharmaceutical firm. There were piles of money to be made—and the risk was much lower. Perhaps in the future, René said, although the request itself was no surprise. Their second request *was* a surprise: They asked him to become Catholic. This stung, but on consideration, René, whose father was Jewish and mother Catholic and whose only religion in his own life was motor racing, agreed.

Then, all of a sudden, Monsieur Miraton died, of a heart attack. He was alone at his dining-room table when he succumbed, cigarette in hand. René and Chou-Chou decided to proceed with their wedding as scheduled, a few days after the funeral. René wore his black funeral suit, Chou-Chou, a black dress. She cried through the ceremony. It was an ill omen for their future together—at a time when the world was full of ill omens.

CHAPTER 15

Six months later, in May 1935, drivers on their way to the Tripoli Grand Prix in Libya gathered in the bar on the ferry across the Mediterranean, sharing memories and laughter. René was there, with Nuvolari and Chiron, his new Scuderia Ferrari teammates. Manfred von Brauchitsch and Luigi Fagioli from Mercedes stood across from their chief rivals of the new season, Auto Union's Hans Stuck and new team member Achille Varzi. For a brief moment, they enjoyed the camaraderie that had been typical in years past.

Preferring to be alone, Rudi snuck away. It was a starless night, and sheets of rain swept across the deck. He lingered beside the W25s, which were draped with gray tarpaulins, and thought of Charly. He had spent the winter away from Switzerland—there were too many memories in the home they had shared. Standing by the railing, he watched the twin rivers of foam-churned sea created by the propellers. He could faintly hear the revelry from the bar and wondered who among them might die in the upcoming race—and what was the point of it all.

In December 1934, the Nazi leadership had made clear what it felt the point was. From a podium at the ministry of propaganda, Adolf Hühnlein addressed racing drivers and Nazi officials: "Racing is and always will be the highest embodiment of motorsport and thus the highest achievement of the nation in any international competition." Rudi and his fellow drivers were certainly all aware of the atrocities the SS and Gestapo were committing against the "enemies of the Reich," which included Jewish people, political opponents, people with disabilities, LGBTQ people, and people of color, but such thoughts were usually best shunted to one side.

Rudi remained on the deck for hours, it seemed, a chill curling around his spine, as he thought of the risk they were taking every time they started their engines. All he knew was that he had no choice but to race, no choice but to sacrifice everything to win, and his only fear was that his body was too weak to compete against a new generation of competitors in ever faster and more powerful cars.

When they docked in Tripoli, the air was vibrating with the heat, and a cloud of red dust cast a pall over the whole city. Horse-drawn carriages took them through the narrow streets, lined with white houses and bustling with people, to the Uaddan Hotel & Casino.

A protectorate of Italy—or its "fourth shore"—Libya was overseen by Governor Italo Balbo, a former Italian air marshal. Balbo loved racing, and under his theatrical touch and Mussolini's favor, the Tripoli Grand Prix became one of the richest, most extravagantly celebrated races. The huge cantilevered grandstand at the Mellaha course was a showstopper in its own right, and the 8.14-mile circuit—a roughly shaped quadrilateral—threaded across salt fields, alongside the Mediterranean, past a sparkling blue lake, and around sand dunes and palm groves.

Unloading the W25 from the ferry in Tripoli's port, 1935.

The course allowed drivers to push flat out along the long, gentle bends. This made it very dangerous for any driver who misjudged the sideways slide of his wheels in bends generally taken at speeds above 140 mph. Noting that this type of controlled drift required "a fine sense of balance and touch and most discriminate use of the throttle, not to mention split-second timing and a very cool head," George Monkhouse, a motorsport writer of the time, added that only a few drivers were capable of executing the maneuver.

From the very start, the race lived up to its billing as the "fastest road circuit in the world." The French and Italian factory teams were largely left behind by the Silver Arrows. The course, subject to the desert heat, shredded the cars' tires and caused the leaderboard to change continually as drivers were forced into the pits one after the other. First Fagioli. Then Caracciola. Then Varzi. Then Stuck.

Rudi suffered three tire failures, but the Mercedes crews had reduced the average time of their pit stops, including refueling stops, from over 2 minutes to 40 seconds—often less. It was a military-style operation, with every move planned, coordinated, and drilled a thousand times.

When a Mercedes driver needed to come into the pits, Neubauer waved a white flag emblazoned with a red cross. The driver killed his engine 120 yards away to keep the spark plugs from mucking up with oil. Momentum carried the silent W25 into the pits, where the driver braked on an exact mark. Any straying from the line—an inch forward or back—cost precious seconds because the tire jacks, pressurized fuel hoses, spare tires, and starters were all prepositioned.

Then three mechanics launched into action. Neubauer had designated the tasks for each of them. "[Mechanic] No. 1 gets the left rear wheel ready while No. 3 hands the driver clean goggles, a piece of chamois to clean the windshield and a glass of water. Then he puts in the fuel. In the meantime, Mechanics No. 1 and 2 have jacked up the car and changed the rear wheels. Mechanic No. 1 has the electric start ready and the engine roars into life."

Throughout, the team manager conferred with his driver, informing him of the state of the race—liberally mixed with plenty of praise about his driving to boost his morale. The speed of the operation gave them a huge advantage over the competition: Rudi called it "the secret of victory." Helping as well was the fact that scores of their engineers and mechanics had worked throughout the past winter to improve the power and reliability of the W25.

With five laps remaining, Varzi was leading for Auto Union, with Rudi in second position, a couple of minutes behind him. Rudi knew that the Italian had pushed too hard, too fast. Rudi just needed to bide his time. Two laps later, the heat vicious on their tires, Varzi threw a tread and pulled in for an emergency pit stop. By the time he returned to the track, Rudi had caught up to within a few car lengths. He patiently remained tethered there until he saw his opportunity, then sped away into the lead.

Nobody was even close as Rudi shot down the ocean side to the finish. He killed the engine and lifted his goggles from his face. Neubauer tap-danced across the pavement, then pulled Rudi free of the W25. A pair of mechanics lifted him onto their shoulders. Everyone wanted to slap him on the back or shake his hand.

He had won.

"There was the sun, the people . . . everything was good and bright and friendly, and I was back," Rudi later wrote. "Yes, that was the greatest marvel. I was back, and I could fight again as well as all the rest . . . the shadow was gone."

A month later, in mid-June, Rudi returned to the Nürburgring for the Eifel race. Three laps from the finish, Bernd Rosemeyer

Rudi victorious in Tripoli, 1935.

from Auto Union took the lead from Rudi, right in front of the grandstands. A former motorcycle racer, the new driver on the scene was twenty-five years old, tall, blond, and handsome. With a smile that could be measured in watts, he was also cocksure, daring, and a natural behind the wheel.

This was Rosemeyer's first season at Auto Union, and only his second race as a Grand Prix driver, but he was already besting the field on a notoriously challenging course in a car that was even more notoriously difficult to handle, particularly in corners where the weight of its rear engine often led to tailspins.

Rudi stuck close to him, studying his every move. Finally, he spotted a weakness in his young rival's management of the course. Near the end of circuit, Rosemeyer always prematurely shifted into fifth gear while coming out of a swallowtail-shaped turn. In the final lap, Rudi remained in fourth gear a spell longer, then stamped on his accelerator. As they exited the turn, Rosemeyer tried to block him out, but it was no use. Fist raised, Rudi crossed the finish first.

In the pits, he stood on the seat of his car, head and shoulders above the crowd that pressed around him. A sea of arms whipped upward in Sieg Heil salutes to the winner. As was expected of him, Rudi followed with his own salute, and his victory became a celebration of the Third Reich—no matter that he considered the victory his, and his alone.

At the postrace party in the Eifelerhof Hotel, Rudi watched everyone congratulate the rookie driver on his "arrival." Rosemeyer was exactly the kind of up-and-comer Rudi feared. To get into his rival's head, the veteran champion pulled the swirl stick from his cocktail and approached Rosemeyer at his table. "Well done, my dear boy, but in the future don't be content to just drive around the circuit. Use your head." Rudi handed him the swirl stick. "With this, you can practice changing gears." Rosemeyer was stone-faced, and a bitter feud was born.

It was a darker, more ruthless Rudi who had returned to the heights of the racing world. He was more vainglorious as well. At the time, one journalist joked that everyone needed a ladder to speak to the German champion.

CHAPTER 16

The meteoric rise of the Silver Arrows had left few victories for anyone else that season. At Monaco, Luigi Fagioli won in his W25. At AVUS, the silver squadrons swept 1-2-3, with Rudi winning again. At the French Grand Prix, the organizers added some chicanes to the Montlhéry road course to slow speeds down and give some advantage to skill. Rudi won anyway. Brauchitsch came in second.

The Grand Prix was another debacle for the French. Not a single French make and not a single French driver even finished the race. A newspaper cartoon showed Mercedes mechanics doing cartwheels in the pits while Rudi Caracciola looked out over a graveyard of French cars. Charles Faroux declared the result "the great misery of French automobile construction." *L'Intransigent*'s Georges Fraichard wrote about the "painful lessons" of the German victory: "When will it be understood in France that it is high time to react?" he asked.

The ACF took the coward's path, announcing its intention to run the 1936 French Grand Prix as a sports-cars-only event. To avoid French cars being trounced again, formula models like the Silver Arrows would not be allowed to compete. Superchargers were banned, and entrants had to be two-seaters fitted with fenders, windshields, horns, rearview mirrors, and complete electric systems, including lights.

Rudi wins the 1935 French Grand Prix.

At the Belgian Grand Prix, René Dreyfus found himself battling against the Germans again. Try as he might to cut their lead in the turns, he could never get in front of them—their acceleration was unmatchable. After the race, it was Rudi on top of the victory stand again, enjoying an *annus mirabilis* after his long recovery.

At the Belgian Grand Prix, run at the Spa-Francorchamps circuit on the edge of the Ardennes, René spent so much time at the Silver Arrows' heels that he grew sick from the noxious exhaust fumes and had to bow out in lap 31. He stretched out on the pavement in the pits to gather himself. Later, eyes still burning, he bathed his face in milk and drank a glass of the same to soothe his throat. His failed effort to beat the field of German cars was not so easily cleared away.

It was only at those races the Germans declined to attend, notably at Pau, Marne, and Dieppe, that Scuderia Ferrari had a shot. Nuvolari won at Pau, and René in the other two in tight finishes against Louis Chiron.

René was glad to be on the Scuderia. First, he and his old friend Louis Chiron were teammates. Second, he greatly admired and liked Nuvolari, who, at forty-three, had lost none of his reflexes or his will to race. There was much to learn from him both on and off the track. Five feet, five inches tall, Nuvolari was reed-thin, with sinewy muscles drawn tightly over his bones. Below his cropped black and gray hair, he had the kind of face that

haunted his competitors: deep hooded eyes, a wide long-toothed smile, a granite chin, and the inability to mask any emotion. Not that he ever tried. Nuvolari was completely without artifice.

"The Flying Mantuan," Tazio Nuvolari, at the German Grand Prix 1935, urging his pit crew to go faster!

He also lacked a sense of caution. During his races, he screamed, beat the sides of his car, and rocked about the cockpit like he could will the machine to go faster. Using his innate sense of balance and dexterity, he slewed around corners at unparalleled speeds, virtually inventing the four-wheel drift. "He drove like a madman, crashing often, flogging his cars as if they were beasts of burden," one historian wrote. "He was, in the argot of the day, the classic *garabaldino*—a driver with the slashing, all-out style of a winner; a charger who drove with such abandon that rumors spread through the crowds that he was haunted by a death wish or, like Paganini, had a pact with the Devil."

Meo Costantini had said to René that he lacked aggressiveness; in that arena, Nuvolari was the foremost professor.

With several wins and top finishes in the seven *Grandes Épreuves* of the season, Rudi won the overall European Championship in 1935. His Mercedes teammates Fagioli and Brauchitsch followed in second and third. Nuvolari was fourth. René finished fifth, with a pair of wins as well as a healthy sequence of second-, third-, and fourth-place results.

The annual shuffle of drivers between teams started soon after. René felt confident that he would be invited to return to the Scuderia the following season, and Ferrari confirmed that he wanted him back. But very swiftly, political winds made his return impossible. Mussolini demanded an all-Italian team, and sentiment in the country was against having a French driver in the red colors, let alone one of Jewish parentage who bore the surname Dreyfus.

It did not matter whether René practiced the Jewish faith. Although his father came from a conservative Jewish family, he did not attend synagogue, and René was never bar mitzvahed. But as his brother Maurice, who also converted to Catholicism on his marriage, was told by an anti-Semite, "Your name is Dreyfus; therefore you are a Jew."

France had deep seams of anti-Semitism that pervaded its culture, seen most pointedly in the trial of French army captain Alfred Dreyfus in 1895. Against clear evidence, Dreyfus was wrongly accused of selling military secrets to Germany and convicted of treason. After much scandal and division, he was later fully cleared of wrongdoing. The "Dreyfus Affair" was far from ancient history in the 1930s, and prejudice against the small population of Jews in France remained typical. Jews may have had French passports, but they were viewed as "other" by many of their compatriots.

Despite this underlying anti-Semitism, and even though René shared a surname with the most famous Jew in France (they were not related), he had rarely faced prejudice in his life. If anything, he had a closer association with his mother's lapsed Catholicism by virtue of the fact that he and his siblings spent more time with her side of the family. Neither religion made any impression on him, and he might have called himself an atheist if he had given any thought to it, but he hadn't. As a driver, his heritage had never affected his prospects, nor had he imagined that it ever would, until Ferrari called René in for a meeting at the Modena headquarters.

Fumes filled the air of the small thirty-man shop that Enzo Ferrari operated from his provincial hometown. The screech of metal being ground or milled made such a din, there was not much his team manager was able to say, nor René to hear. The gist was that it was best he return to France to drive for a French team. René accepted it, even though he hated it. He and Chou-Chou packed up and returned to Paris.

At the same time, René learned that Mercedes had signed Louis Chiron, in part because of the recruitment efforts of Rudi Caracciola. This was a further blow to René. It was clear to everyone that his 1935 record was far superior to that of Chiron. Many believed that, given the right car, René could have been one of the top three drivers on the circuit. If anybody (apart from Nuvolari, who was forced by Mussolini's government to remain with Ferrari) deserved a spot with Mercedes, the best team in Europe, it was René. The implication was again obvious: René was Jewish, and a Jewish driver could not represent the Mercedes or Auto Union Silver Arrows.

Over at Auto Union, Hans Stuck was almost removed from the team because he was married to tennis star Paula von Reznicek, whose grandfather was Jewish. Only Stuck's close association with Hitler saved him from banishment. Adolf Rosenberger, the sole prominent German Jewish driver, was not so fortunate, even though he had helped fund Porsche in the early development of the P-Wagen. Rosenberger was forbidden a license to compete, arrested by the SS for "racial disgrace" (code for having relations with an Aryan), and beaten in a concentration camp before he fled to America.

René heard that Neubauer considered hiring him at one point. When it was pointed out to him that the French driver was the son of a Jew, Neubauer tartly responded, "They will decide who's Jewish." (*They* meant Hitler.) It seemed that sometimes, when it suited him, Hitler would overlook a person's heritage. But the fact was that, as with Rosenberger, Hitler would never allow a Dreyfus to race under the Nazi banner.

René knew that he had few choices of team, if any, if he wanted to take part in the 1936 Grand Prix circuit. He was a jockey without a horse. That October, he attended the annual ACF dinner in Paris. Surrounded by the who's who of international motor racing, including a delegation from the NSKK, he endured the medal presentation to Rudi Caracciola for his "splendid" French Grand Prix win and then long-winded speeches by one elderly, tuxedoed ACF official after another.

One spoke about how the League of Nations would surely guarantee peace in Europe. Another praised the Germans for their "magnificent success," avoiding any mention of their obvious government support. A third lamented the lack of a decent French car, particularly since Bugatti had said that it would probably not be competing the following year. "Are we going to resign ourselves to the decline of our colors?" he asked. No one mentioned how the ugly political landscape had cast some drivers adrift while benefiting others greatly. Seated together at the dinner, René and Rudi embodied that divide.

PART III

THE MILLION

CHAPTER 17

With a jubilant shout of *"Partez!"* Lucy Schell launched her Delahaye 135 down the palm-tree-lined road from Athens to Eleusis in Greece. It was January 25, 1936, and her and Laury's Monte Carlo Rally had officially begun. Behind them, the moonlit ruins of the Acropolis faded in the distance.

The two-seater convertible roadster was the first of its kind. Under the curved lines of its coachwork, designed by Joseph Figoni, was a tiger of an engine. At 3.5 liters, it was as sturdy as its predecessor but threw out a lot more horsepower. Jean François had fitted it on an altered chassis, with a long wheelbase that sat even lower to the ground. He had also improved its suspension. Compared to some of the boneshakers Lucy had driven, the Delahaye was a balanced and smooth ride.

Before François finished the build, Lucy visited Weiffenbach at the Delahaye factory to order a dozen for herself and her friends. "There you are, Monsieur Charles. My order will cover the cost of the pair you want to run yourself. Now will you please ask François to do what he can for us?" As a mark of gratitude, Weiffenbach made sure that the very first 135 completed was delivered to her.

Once out of the Greek capital, the route quickly turned into a dirt trail that threaded past olive groves up into snow-covered mountains. Only 2,400 miles to go before they reached Monaco. Given their experience—and their new car—they believed that this time, victory might be theirs at last and Lucy would make her mark as the first female driver to win the Rally.

The warm weather favored the eighteen competitors who departed from Athens. They easily crossed several mountain passes that most years would have been deep in snow—one of the reasons why that particular route was considered the most challenging. Near Larissa, the road cut through some marshes and low fields where traces of the Great War were still visible: Ragged trench lines scarred the land, and shell craters had left pockmarks on the terrain. It looked like the surface of the moon.

In Bulgaria and Yugoslavia, the roads were little more than muddy ruts, and Lucy had to navigate around gullies and potholes big enough to swallow their car—at speeds that would have made most tremble. The Delahaye handled these perils and the constant shifting of gears as if it was enjoying having its engine and its independent front suspension tested and stretched.

The tires clung to the road around bends, and the car practically leaped forward on the straights, its almost noiseless six-cylinder engine begging to be allowed to run free at its maximum speed of 115 mph. The cable brakes were sturdy, and the steering was as precise as a surgeon's blade. When a journalist at *Autocar* got his hands on the car later that year, he praised it unreservedly: "The whole machine is responsive, almost alive, so exactly does the engine answer the driver's ideas of what he wants to do in relation to other traffic and to the actual road conditions, so

XVIᴱ RALLYE INTERNATIONAL DE
MONTE CARLO

PREMIER
DU CLASSEMENT GÉNÉRAL
à ce véritable championnat
du monde de grand tourisme
PREMIER
de l'épreuve d'accélération, de
freinage et de maniabilité,
LE TYPE 135 SPORT
DELAHAYE
confirme une fois de plus ses
qualités incontestables de
VITESSE - MANIABILITÉ
SOUPLESSE - ROBUSTESSE

DELAHAYE

exactly do the controls perform the necessary operations."

When the Schells reached Hungary, they tore down the well-kept roads toward Budapest. From there they ventured on to Vienna through a fog so thick they didn't realize night had fallen. Snow fell on the way to Salzburg, but the Delahaye kept to the road without needing chains. Several days—and almost a thousand miles—after that, they entered Monte Carlo, right on schedule.

The performance test involved a figure-eight course featuring two pylons that had to be rounded at flat-out speed. The Schells posted a time of 1 minute 5.4 seconds, trouncing those who had gone before. One after another, their fellow competitors failed to match their speed, and it looked like they might have the Rally in the bag.

Then Romanian driver Petre Cristea shot around the course in his Ford in 1 minute 5 seconds flat. When his time was announced, the Schells blanched. Long-sought victory had been swept out from under them. They had to settle for second place.

At almost forty years of age, Lucy knew that her chances of being the first woman to win the Monte Carlo Rally were now slim. It was time to move on, time to find other goals. It was true that she had already founded her own sports-car racing team. She had the money and, after years organizing her own participation at events, she certainly had the experience to run such an organization. Two events—one in motorsport, the other on the global stage—brought an even grander goal right into her sights.

On February 15, the AIACR Sports Commission had declared the results of its winter deliberations on the new Grand Prix formula for 1937 to 1939. The previous formula, with its 750-kilogram maximum weight limit, had failed to control speeds and had only led to the dominance of the German manufacturers. Every year their engines grew bigger and more powerful. The new formula aimed to limit engine capacity to lower speeds and to allow for a broader range of car sizes, opening up the sport to more manufacturers.

Faroux, the wise old man of French motorsport, considered the revised formula a travesty. With their bottomless funds, the Germans were sure to produce supercharged engines vastly more powerful than expected. Given the amount and type of fuel these would burn, not to mention the design complexity, he wrote, such racing cars would "no longer be automobiles." He lamented that his country had no means to challenge the state-funded Silver Arrows, despite his best efforts in that regard.

After the debacle of the 1934 French Grand Prix, to save his country's Grand Prix hopes from "the abyss," Faroux had proposed the Fonds de Course, a subscription fund that would help French manufacturers build a winning Grand Prix car. He suggested a 10-franc fee be charged on every driving license issued in the country and the money given to French firms. In December 1935, the government approved the measure of a "Million Franc" fund, but it would take a year to raise the monies, and by then, it would be too late to finance a race car that used the new formula for the 1937 season.

When Lucy read Faroux's piece in *L'Auto*, she knew something must be done—and that she was in a position to do it.

The other event that focused Lucy's mind was Nazi Germany's occupation of the demilitarized Rhineland in March 1936. This act tore to shreds the Treaty of Versailles, the peace treaty between the Allies and Germany after World War I. Through her service as a nurse during the war, Lucy had seen what devastation an aggressive Germany could wreak on Europe. She had tended the wounds and the misery of innumerable Allied soldiers who had fallen in battle against them. Consequently, there was no love lost between her and Germany. Furthermore, the Silver Arrows had wrecked any chance at victory in motor racing by a French-made car and had fueled the propaganda machine of the Nazi regime.

Lucy made a decision. The time had come to step away from her own career as a driver and to concentrate her full attention on running her own motorsport team. She would never be the first woman to win the Monte Carlo Rally, so why not be the first woman to command a team in the Grand Prix? What was more, and more important, she later told *Paris Soir*, she aimed to bolster "French prestige" and to show the Nazis that their days of unrivaled dominance in motorsport were numbered. After all, nobody else was stepping forward to challenge them.

Taking the, by now, well-beaten path to the rue du Banquier, Lucy paid Charles Weiffenbach a visit. "What is it now, Madame Schell?" he asked. "Your next two cars are nearly ready; we are all soon gathering at Montlhéry for a public demonstration... What more can Delahaye do for you?"

"Very simple, Monsieur Charles!" Lucy declared. "You can build me a 4.5-liter racing car for the 1937 formula. I've decided to run a team in the Grand Prix."

Weiffenbach was speechless.

"They will be my cars," Lucy continued. "I will finance the project from top to bottom: design, construction, development, the racing itself. I'm offering you an opportunity which I'm sure isn't available to any other firm in France. Now, what do you say?"

If anybody else had asked the Delahaye production chief to build a Grand Prix car from scratch, he would have laughed them out of his office. He was a businessman, and back in 1932, when lead board member Marguerite Desmarais had instructed him to build cars that won races, what she meant was to build sports cars that people might then buy to take out on the open road. Grand Prix cars were too powerful and temperamental for the average driver to handle. Further, they were very expensive to design, produce, and maintain over a season. Firms like Daimler-Benz and Auto Union could afford such investments. They were massive industrial corporations with multiple plants, legions of engineers, vast sums of money, and strong government support. Compared to them, Delahaye was a Lilliputian.

But Weiffenbach recognized an opportunity when it crossed his path. Lucy's idea might have been outlandish, but her financial support meant that developing a Grand Prix design would not cost his company a single franc. If they managed to produce a worthy car, the publicity alone would provide a bonanza unlike

Lucy Schell looking keenly into the future.

any since the board charged him with making the marque better known. He liked the idea of returning France to where he saw as its rightful place in motorsport.

Then Lucy told him the name she had chosen for the team: Écurie Bleue (the "Blue Team"). Blue was the color that traditionally represented France, back to the early days of the monarchy. The patriotic name sealed the deal for Monsieur Charles. He asked Jean François to begin development straight away.

While Weiffenbach was excited about competing on the Grand Prix circuit, that did not mean he had abandoned reason. Any design was worth doing only if it could be put into production as a car that the general public would buy. A supercharged engine would be of little use in a regular Delahaye production model, not least because of its high fuel consumption. They had no experience designing such blown engines and knew that it was bound to be a very costly, time-consuming exercise. Lucy Schell might have deep pockets, but they were not limitless.

François proposed a V12** unsupercharged engine sized to the formula's maximum capacity of 4.5 liters. Weiffenbach added that it had to be lightweight, efficient, durable, easy to manufacture or fix, and it had to run on regular gas. François got to work.

Over the next few days, François had long working lunches at the Restaurant Duplantin, sketching designs in his notebook.

....

** V12 signifies a twelve-cylinder engine, with two banks of six cylinders situated at an angle toward one another, just like the two sides of a V.

The bustle of life on the Place Péreire outside might as well have disappeared as he worked out his rough plans in pencil. Sometimes he became so excited that he scribbled on the white tablecloth. They were only drawings—and only of the engine. The chassis, suspension, brakes, steering, aerodynamic body, and a thousand other considerations had to be decided. But it was a purposeful start.

CHAPTER 18

A blanket of fog settled over the Ring during the seventh lap of the Eifel race, on June 14, and the Nürburg castle disappeared in the white cloud. The mist spread across the grandstands, and the scoreboard and signal system faded away. Visibility on the roller-coaster mountain course dropped to fifty yards. Bernd Rosemeyer maintained his speed through the blind twists, distancing himself from his closest competitor, Nuvolari in a red Alfa.

The crowds lining the course heard the thunder of the Auto Union V16 engine. Then, all of a sudden, the silver car broke through the wall of fog only to vanish just as quickly. "It must be a drive of amazing peril, groping through the clouds, in the mountains," *Autocar* reported. At the finish, the writer continued, "No one can see the approach of the cars. The staccato bark of the Auto Union is heard at last, and the crowd cheers Rosemeyer to the echo."

The win was the young competitor's first of the 1936 season, and his driving mesmerized all who witnessed it. Racing journalists called him "Der Nebelmeister" ("the Fog Master"), echoing the nickname Der Regenmeister that Rudi had earned at his rainy triumph at AVUS a decade before. Afterward, Bernd's jovial smile beamed from the newsstands, and profiles of the "thunderbolt known as Rosemeyer" spun from the presses.

Bernd Rosemeyer on the Ring in his rear-engine P-Wagen, 1936.

Bernd had been watching automobiles get disassembled in his father's garage since the time he could crawl. At the age of nine, he was so eager to drive that his parents fixed wood blocks to the pedals of a car and let him have a go. By sixteen, he had saved enough pocket money to buy his first motorcycle. His persistent speeding around the town caused the police to revoke his license.

In the spring of 1934, Auto Union recruited him to its motorcycle team. Many victories followed. That fall, they invited him to try out for the race-car team. Despite having never driven a Grand Prix car, he finished with the second-fastest time and earned a spot on the team. With his fast reflexes, ferocious

Bernd with his wife, Elly Beinhorn, and Auto Union engineer Ferdinand Porsche.

driving style, and natural balance behind the wheel, Bernd reminded many of Tazio Nuvolari. Bernd won his first Grand Prix race in the last event of his rookie season, the 1935 Czechoslovakian Grand Prix, run at the Masaryk circuit outside Brno on September 29. At the celebration party afterward, he met and fell in love with aviator Elly Beinhorn. Already famous, the twenty-eight-year-old was giving a talk in the Czech city about her latest aerial expedition. Always in a rush, Bernd asked her to marry him soon after meeting her. The newspapers labeled them "the fastest couple in the world." In July 1936, a month after he won at the Nürburgring, Bernd and Elly wed.

Rosemeyer was the living embodiment of the Nazi ideal. As historian Anthony Pritchard remarked, "If [he] had not existed, then the National Socialist Party would have had to invent him." While he was racing motorcycles, he had worn a swastika armband, and like many ambitious young men, he had joined the SS. As a reward for his Eifel race victory, Heinrich Himmler personally promoted him to Obersturmführer ("senior leader").

Rudi Caracciola continued to be Germany's best driver, but in comparison to Bernd, he was a crippled old veteran. Bernd was, the newspapers spun, "the radiant boy," a "bold fighter" as well as "a man of action," "risky but self-assured." His looks, the Aryan ideal from head to foot, did not go unremarked: "Beautiful blond Bernd" was a charming rascal, one report went. "Unforgettable, dazzling Bernd, the young Siegfried among the racing aces in the world," gushed another.

With his wife, Elly, the convention-breaking "German

heroine" who had survived a crash landing in the Sahara Desert and who had flown solo from Europe to Australia, they were a fairy tale of the Reich, proof of the superiority of "Aryan blood." The dashing race-car driver and adventurous aviator were seen as Das Traumpaar ("the perfect couple").

Thirteen days after Bernd and Elly's marriage, Rudi faced his rival at the German Grand Prix. Bernd took a significant lead by the first half of the race and was never challenged. He spent his final lap waving at his adoring fans and finished four minutes ahead of his closest competitor. In front of photographers, he sealed his commanding triumph with a kiss from Elly. An exuberant Korpsführer Hühnlein presented him with the trophy and a laurel wreath.

Throughout the award ceremony, Rudi stood grimly beside Bernd.

CHAPTER 19

In the spring of 1936, René Dreyfus was working for the fledgling Talbot-Lago automobile company. The previous fall, with no other options, he agreed to become their race-team captain. He spent most of his time in their well-appointed offices in a suburb west of Paris. While his racing brethren were preparing for the new season, he was wearing a suit and a tie and working on putting together a factory team that could compete in sports-car races.

Whenever anyone asked, he was positive about Talbot's prospects: He only needed to hire one more driver; their new car was handling well; their schedule of events was all set. "We still have a lot to do," he declared brightly to a reporter.

The reality was that he had been forced to hire and babysit an inexperienced driver named Jimmy Bradley solely because he was the son of the *Autocar* editor. Worse, and much more troublesome, Talbot's sports car, a four-liter version of their six-cylinder T150, remained hampered by mechanical trouble.

On May 24, René changed his business suit for overalls to compete in his first competition for Talbot: the Three Hours of Marseille. His blue T150 had been fitted with mudguards and lights to match the sports-car specifications. At the Miramas autodrome, he and his fellow Talbot driver, André Morel, faced ten Delahaye 135s and a Bugatti to see who could cover the greatest distance around the track in three hours. Two of the Delahayes were fielded by its factory team, and three by Lucy Schell's team, including one piloted by husband, Laury.

Before the race started, Talbot's owner, Tony Lago, pulled René aside. "Just go as fast as you can," he said. "It's okay if you break down." They both knew their cars were unreliable, and all Lago wanted to achieve from the race was to prove that Talbot was back in the game.

René followed the orders he had been given—and then some. After the first round of the five-kilometer circuit, he was leading by 300 meters. He clocked a lap record, hitting speeds of over 125 mph. After the fifth lap, he retired with engine trouble. Morel suffered the same and bowed out too.

Delahaye dominated, their factory driver Michael Paris (the racing name for Henri Toulouse) winning the race, with Laury Schell in second place. People were beginning to take notice of Delahaye and Lucy Schell's team, including René Dreyfus.

To design any car, let alone a Grand Prix competitor that might combat Mercedes and Auto Union, demanded many things: the imaginative leaps of an artist; the deductive patience of a mechanic; knowledge about metallurgy, electricity, physics, mathematics, aerodynamics, production; and, of course, engineering. Jean François had all of these—as well as a strong dose of practicality.

Everything started with the engine. A V12 was the obvious

choice, even though Delahaye had not built one since its boat-racing days. Although V12s were complex to build, they generally ran more smoothly, allowed for higher engine speed, and delivered more power than a six-cylinder engine of similar capacity. One driver described the V12 as delivering "a peculiar pulse that is the sonic equivalent of strawberry mousse and cream." There was simply something smooth and luscious about it.

François set the two six-cylinder banks at a sixty-degree angle to one another. To feed fuel and air into the 4.5-liter engine, he designed the camshaft in a way that allowed the engine to breathe better and operate more efficiently. He also decided to cast the one-piece engine block in magnesium alloy instead of traditional aluminum, reducing its weight by 35 percent. François's simple early sketches turned into scores of blueprints until he had finished plans ready to send to the factory floor.

Regardless of how well built and tuned the engine, François knew that his 4.5-liter design would produce a maximum of 225–250 hp, a measurement almost half of what the Germans would likely churn out of a 3-liter, supercharged engine, particularly one operating on a custom fuel mix. But Monsieur Charles wanted an engine that could be installed in everything from a Grand Prix competitor, to a sports car, to a high-end coupé used for outings about the city or countryside. That was the Delahaye way. The 145 would have efficiency, versatility, and toughness on its side. In a long race, these were qualities to be prized.

Any engine was useless without a chassis that could nimbly handle the road. In his design, François mirrored closely that of

Illustration of a V12 engine.

the 135—its innovative leaps had resulted in a command of everything from oval tracks to mountain climbs. A two-seater of rigid construction, the chassis sat a bit lower and ran slightly longer than its predecessor. But these were minor differences. They shared a similar independent front suspension, cable-operated brakes, and an engine position that distributed the car's weight evenly. "No wild innovations here," one critic would write. "Just well-polished state-of-art logic as a foundation for refined tuning, development, and durability." Delahaye lacked an in-house coach-building operation, but it was intended that the car's body be lightweight and utilitarian.

The factory had four 145s on order from Écurie Bleue. Building them had been slow because of widespread strikes and industrial unrest in 1936, but the first chassis was on course to be assembled by late fall, and the company expected to have an engine ready for testing in early 1937. The finished cars, weighing roughly 850 kilograms (1,875 pounds) to meet the formula minimum weight, were to be ready by late spring.

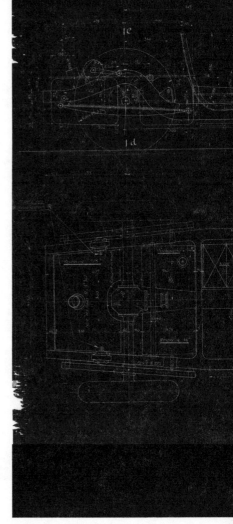

Lucy handled the drivers, managed the partnership with Delahaye, built out an organization of mechanics and support staff, and bankrolled the whole affair. The team now had its own garage, a two-car transport truck, and a mobile machine shop. There was much to show for her efforts. Her two best drivers—Laury and Joseph Paul—ranked well at several sports-car events in France.

Blueprint of the Delahaye 145 design.

Now it was time to find a worthy driver—a champion—to lead her assault on the Grand Prix. Such drivers were few in number, and fewer still were those not already committed to established teams. She needed someone who would be prepared not only to take orders from a woman but also to drive for a fledgling team whose cars were still in development. She needed someone desperate, someone eager to prove or to reestablish themself. One name, and one name alone, came to mind: René Dreyfus.

Anyone could see that he was not happy at Talbot. There was no place for him at Bugatti. Neither the Italians nor Germans would have him. She had seen him race dozens of times, and he was what most of the press said: a driver with "finesse and intelligence," someone of "great precision who could teach a class on holding a line." As a competitor, he was "calm, measured of movement, and patient as an angel."

René may have been down on his luck, but he had driven for most of the greats: Bugatti, Maserati, and Alfa Romeo. He had called teammate many of the fastest drivers in the world. Lucy knew he had the skill to win any race, but the question was whether he had the fire. Well, she was nothing if not a fire-starter.

She knew she would have to convince him, and, indeed, when they finally met in the autumn of 1936 at her house, she bowled him over with her energy and enthusiasm and her promises about what might be if he agreed to drive for her. He would have a salary, his choice of other drivers, and the freedom to help develop and test-drive the new car. Together, they could bring France back into the winners' circle and pierce the invincibility of the German Silver Arrows.

Neither of them recorded what else was said that day. Perhaps Lucy told René about always being the outsider looking to make good—not French enough in France, not American enough in America; the nouveau riche upstart in a class-conscious Europe;

a woman in a sport ruled by men; a wife and mother who preferred the garage and the racetrack to the conventional hearth and home. No doubt she could tell him a thousand tales about malign looks and whispered comments.

Perhaps she called to his attention the fact that he was an outsider too. She knew he had been forced off the Ferrari team. She knew the Germans would never take him. All his skill and experience meant little when balanced against the name Dreyfus. It did not matter whether he saw himself as a Jew. They did—all the more so because he was the only one in the Grand Prix. Even if he did not hear the slights or see the looks, they happened nonetheless.

Together, they could tip the scales in their favor, the outsiders atop the Grand Prix. Imagine it. The journey would not be easy. He would have to rediscover the fierceness of his early La Turbie days, as well as the fearlessness that first catapulted him into the Grand Prix with his 1930 Monaco win. Whether Lucy spoke of all or none of this, whether she needed to or not, René was persuaded by this fascinating lady "who talked a very good story." In the end, as usual, Lucy got her way.

On December 10, 1936, everybody in the motorsport world knew about Lucy's offer and René's decision when, a few days after the definitive AIACR ruling on the new formula was finally made, Charles Weiffenbach and Lucy Schell announced Écurie Bleue at a press conference. The team would, Weiffenbach declared, represent Delahaye in all sports-car competitions the following year, and it would field a car in the Grand Prix in 1938. Lucy Schell would be the boss of the whole affair and René Dreyfus the premier driver.

CHAPTER 20

In mid-January 1937, René headed to the German port city of Hamburg to begin his first adventure with Écurie Bleue. Lucy wanted him to make his debut for the team in a competition he had never run before: the Monte Carlo Rally. He would partner with Laury in one of their Delahaye 135s.

Initially, René was reluctant. He was a race-car driver, not a rallyer—a distinctly different breed. But after some consideration, he decided that the whole affair would be a fun escapade. The average speed of 25 mph over the route seemed like it would make for an easy "long walk" over the 2,300 miles to Monte Carlo, especially since he was used to maneuvering through packs of cars at quadruple that speed on narrower courses. He would see some beautiful scenery along the way and was looking forward to competing with Laury, who loved cars even more than he did.

In Hamburg, René took the wheel of the canvas-topped Delahaye 135, and he and Laury headed to their starting point in Stavanger, Norway, a journey of 1,000 miles. At the Danish border, they were faced with a wall of snow. A blizzard raged across northern Europe, making roads impassable. After retreating to Hamburg, they boarded the cargo ship *Venus* to reach the west coast of Norway.

René spent the journey curled up in his seat, his face white and his stomach roiling like the deck underneath him. Outside, a dry, icy wind howled, and foam-flecked waves slammed against the hull. All of the North Sea looked like it had risen up to send him to its black depths. Ships were sinking or foundering up and down the Norwegian coastline, and at one point, theirs needed to stop to assist a vessel and take on its passengers.

Laury, who had the constitution of a grizzled sailor, thought René needed to buck up. He promised him that there would be more trouble ahead once they reached firm ground.

By the time they arrived in Stavanger, they rushed to make the start. Neither had slept or eaten in almost a day. Still, at 1 p.m. on January 26, sporting a fur-lined black leather trench coat, René was excited to be at the starting line. Everybody—from the organizers to the local people to the thirty driver teams—was friendly and enthusiastic, particularly since the sun had come out.

René made quick work over the first hour, averaging 40 mph. He liked how the little Delahaye drove. What its engine lacked in power, it made up for in quickness; the brakes were tight, and its steering was responsive. The car just felt right. Then the road slickened into a skating rink, buffeted by ferocious winds. René slowed, but he found that the 135 persisted in shearing out from under him, something he had never experienced while learning to drive around the sun-kissed streets of the Riviera.

He and Laury put chains on the tires to increase their grip, but the road ahead only got worse. On the first leg to the control point in Kristiansand, a 185-mile route through a rugged,

René Dreyfus and Laury Schell at the 1937 Monte Carlo Rally.

pine-strewn landscape skirting the Norwegian coast, they passed several competitors stuck in snowbanks. Most were behind schedule. Two decided to abandon the Rally altogether.

The sky darkened early as René was attacking a high pass. White-knuckling the steering wheel, he struggled to keep

the Delahaye on track during the ascent. The sharp slalom of the descent proved trickier, but he avoided disaster. They reached the Kristiansand checkpoint a few minutes ahead of schedule. After a brief break, they returned to a road that looked like it had been carved into a corridor of snow. Its hard-packed walls rose high above their roofline. Any loss of control, and it would be akin to crashing inside a concrete tunnel. René was gaining a newfound respect for Lucy's sporting achievements.

Sixty miles out of Kristiansand, the 135 threw a tire chain, which then twisted around the brake drum. As René and Laury labored in the middle of the night to loosen the chain, the Arctic cold numbed their hands and bit their faces. Ten minutes passed. Then half an hour. Still they struggled to untangle the chain. Competitors slowed to curl around them on the narrow road.

At last they cut it free with pliers. They had fallen almost an hour behind, time they tried to recover over the next 150 miles to Oslo by barreling onward, tires aimed at the grooves carved into the compacted snow by the other competitors. Whenever their wheels abandoned these "tramlines," as they called them, their tail end performed acrobatics.

They arrived six minutes past the control-point deadline and incurred three penalty points. Barring misfortune hitting every team in the race, they had forfeited their chance at a first-place finish. Such were the vagaries of the Rally.

They continued on into Sweden, then down the coastline toward Denmark. René learned to trust the Delahaye and to accept the risk of an accident that came at every turn and downhill sweep of the road. With each hour, he grew more confident.

He was much less assured when it came to navigation. Ice and snow blanketed most signs, and he took several wrong turns while Laury was sleeping that were discovered only after he woke up. At one crossroads, René had lost all confidence in his sense of direction. He elbowed Laury to ask for help. "Which way do you want to turn, René?" Laury asked.

"Left."

"Turn right, René."

This scene repeated itself often. Whatever direction René chose, Laury opted for the opposite, and they began arriving at their checkpoints easily on schedule.

Forty hours after leaving Stavanger, they got a couple of hours of sleep on a Danish ferry. Then it was back to the road. Yawning every few minutes, René continued to drive, wisely coached by a co-driver who was running his eleventh Monte Carlo Rally. "Bet that today you would prefer to be on the starting line of a Grand Prix race," Laury joked as they drove down a slick stretch of French highway where several trucks had slid off the road into ditches. René agreed. In some ways, the Rally was far more dangerous, particularly since that year they were competing during one of the worst winter storms in decades.

René and Laury arrived in Monte Carlo on a hot, clear day that might have been mistaken for summer. They performed well in the series of acceleration and braking tests. They finished fifth overall. Another Delahaye driver, René Le Bègue, won first place.

Lucy was well versed in the trials her new driver had faced, and she, Laury, and René celebrated at the Schells' villa beside the Jardin Exotique de Monaco, high in the hills above the sea. Relaxing by the Mediterranean, René had time to reflect on his journey. He realized now just how hard Lucy intended to push him in the Grand Prix.

In Germany, sporting success was now intertwined with the prestige and power of the nation. A *L'Auto* columnist wrote, "The Age of Sport is now consecrated; deplore it or approve it, but you will not change it." In 1936, the Germans looked unbeatable: from Max Schmeling's twelfth-round knockout of Joe Louis in Yankee Stadium, New York, on June 18; to the eighty-nine medals won by the German athletes at the Summer Olympics in Berlin; to the Silver Arrows' dominance on racetracks across Europe all that summer long.

Rudi Caracciola had come to accept that politics and motor racing were now inseparable. He was ambiguous about the Nazis but knew that if he wanted to compete, he was going to have to play his part as one of their heroes. Whenever he mounted the victory stand, he gave the Nazi salute, and he was happy to appear in Reich propaganda that labeled its Grand Prix drivers "Swift as greyhounds, tough as leather, strong as Krupp steel."

In February, he went to Monza to trial the W125, the latest Mercedes formula car. Mercedes engineer Rudolf Uhlenhaut presented him with a marvel. In only six months, Uhlenhaut had reinvented Mercedes's formula car, a surprising accomplishment for anyone and particularly so for a thirty-year-old mechanical engineer of reserved demeanor and little management experience.

When he was hired as technical director for the Mercedes racing department, Uhlenhaut inherited a team of three hundred engineers, technicians, and mechanics, most of whom were dispirited after the performance of their 1936 design.

Throughout the season, Bernd Rosemeyer and Auto Union had trounced the Mercedes team as it struggled with their redesigned W25s. The engineers had increased its engine size while shortening the wheelbase, which gave the cars a striking look, but race after race, they proved difficult to control and broke down frequently. "Sheep in wolves' clothing," one writer labeled them.

That autumn, to determine the problem, Uhlenhaut had taken a pair of the W25s out around the Nürburgring. To keep the affair quiet, he was accompanied only by a few mechanics. He had never driven a race car, and he started out at a snail's pace, but over the course of the next couple of days and some thousand miles of driving, often at top speeds, he had a better understanding of what he needed to do.

To begin with, he replaced the chassis, which warped and vibrated on uneven roads, with a stronger, oval tubular frame. He lengthened the wheelbase by a foot to provide stability. He improved the brakes and overhauled the suspension, softening the springing and providing much better traction at high speeds.

As for the engine, Uhlenhaut stayed with the straight-eight but increased its capacity significantly to 5.66 liters. In tests at the

Untertürkheim plant, the engine developed an incredible 589 hp. To maintain the 750-kilogram maximum weight, most of the car was built with advanced light-alloy steels.

For several weeks, Rudi trialed the W125. The wheels clung to the road like glue to paper, and it was fast—faster than anything he had ever driven. He reached 88 mph in first gear. In second, 137. In third, 159. In fourth, the top gear, he accelerated to 199 mph. The results elated him. At last he had a new weapon against Bernd Rosemeyer, who had replaced Rudi as European Champion.

Throughout April 1937, Jean François struggled with building his new engine. Early in the new year, Delahaye's foundry had cast the magnesium-alloy cylinder blocks. Using magnesium meant that the block weighed half of what one cast in iron would have weighed. Despite tipping the scales at roughly the same as the 135 engine, the V12 would provide 50 percent more power and turned 1,000 rpm faster. However, when they were cast, the magnesium developed gas bubbles, and when the blocks cooled, their skin was porous, causing leaks.

In late spring, François succeeded in assembling an engine. Then, during tests, other issues arose. Again, the magnesium blocks presented problems, this time because the alloy expanded and contracted at a different rate from the steel in the studs that held it in place. Effectively, the engine tore itself apart when heated up. Dispirited with his progress, François considered abandoning the whole design.

When Monsieur Charles failed in his gruff efforts to spur him onward, Lucy stepped in with words of encouragement and motivation. She was unequivocal: Work until it works. He continued to labor on the engine until every cylinder leak, loose valve, and structural weakness had been fixed.

When the Delahaye 145 was finally revealed at Montlhéry, Lucy did not invite any press to the event. There was a chance the car she had financed might sputter and die; the gearbox might break; the tires might fling off—if recent experience in the 135 was any guide.

Her team had been bedeviled by accidents and mechanical failures that season, leaving Bugatti and Talbot to dominate the French sports-car races. One of the few bright spots was the tenacity of her team captain. At the 24 Hours of Le Mans the week before, René had fallen back to the middle. His co-driver, Henri Stoffel, had broken the door during a pit stop, and the fix had taken almost an hour.

René had told Monsieur Charles that he would claw his way back into position by racing "as if this were a Grand Prix." Then he proceeded to pilot his 135 at a delirious pace for ten hours straight, much of it in the dark, through the flat wheat fields lining the wishbone-shaped course. He placed a remarkable third.

On the afternoon of June 25, the Écurie Bleue transporter rumbled into the Montlhéry autodrome. Lucy was there to greet it, along with René and Jean François. Monsieur Charles and a couple of the Delahaye board members arrived soon after. Apart from this small crew and a couple of track officials, the grounds were empty.

The 145 rolled down the transporter's ramp onto the concrete track. There were no cheers, no champagne corks, barely even a murmur.

Those who had not yet seen the car were shocked by its appearance. The 145 looked nothing like its trim, elegantly shaped predecessor, nor like any other Delahaye they had seen before. Some thought its design must have been inspired by Lucy's bulldogs. Or an electric light bulb tilted on its side. It was called "weird," "brutal," "downright ugly." René thought it "the most awful-looking car [he] ever saw." All that mattered to Lucy was that it ran—and that it ran fast.

François insisted he be the first to test it on the track. As he tucked himself into the cockpit, incongruously dressed in a sport jacket and tie, Georges Fraichard arrived with a photographer. He must have been tipped off. "How is she going to behave?" the *L'Intransigent* reporter asked.

"She has never been driven before," François replied.

His mechanics started the engine. As the V12 took life, a sharp, pulsating rasp broke the almost monastic quiet on the track. François pulled away, switching through the gears, and the pitch of the engine grew deeper, more authoritative, as though it was settling into its own aggressive voice. Any thoughts of the car's ill looks vanished. Turning to Fraichard, René whispered, "She's pretty, is she not? She rides low and gives a beautiful impression of power."

François completed a couple of laps of the oval autodrome, then he gave over the pilot seat to René. On his first lap, he went slowly, then he began to get a feel for the car, the stiffness of the reinforced chassis, the almost featherlight gear change. The steering wheel vibrated from the power of the engine.

Then he pressed his foot down all the way on the accelerator. The Delahaye leaped forward and banked around the autodrome, steady and sure as a ball around a roulette wheel. René covered a lap at 126 mph, then did several more, the engine never exceeding 4,000 rpm. Finally, he pulled up beside the huddle of onlookers and stopped sharply. The brakes were powerful too. There were handshakes and congratulations all around. Lucy was very pleased. Her car ran. It ran very well indeed.

After the celebrations, René returned to the track to put the Delahaye through its paces. A half hour later, the engine overheated. François returned the car to the rue du Banquier and made some refinements. Then the car came back to Montlhéry, and René tested it again. More trouble with ventilation. Back to the factory. More tests. More problems. More modifications.

They were on a rushed schedule—perhaps an impossible one. Their first goal: the Million Franc prize. This was the larger of two prizes put up by the Fonds de Course subscription fund to foster development by a French manufacturer of a Grand Prix car. It would go to whoever completed the fastest 16 laps—200 kilometers—from a standing start at the Montlhéry road circuit by August 31, 1937. The winning car would need to average a speed of 146.5 kph (91 mph).

One million francs. It was a round number, elegant and long, one that sparked immediate interest and played well across newspaper headlines. As one historian enthusiastically wrote, "It was to catch the imagination of the French public as no other motor racing event had succeeded in doing, either before or since: a drama on a national scale playing on some of the deepest human instincts and emotions—passion for sport, admiration of skill and prowess, love of country—and all brought to the boil in a cauldron fired by that most magical of all motivators, lust for money."

Lucy aimed for nothing less than to declare her ownership of the best French race car: first, by winning the Million, probably against the arrogant Bugatti boys, who had been gifted the first of the two prizes without competition, and second, by knocking the Germans off their perch in the following year's Grand Prix formula season.

René doubted they would accomplish even the first of her ambitions. Delahaye's chances of achieving the 146.5 kph average before the deadline of August 31, 1937, or besting any other manufacturer's increase over that average, looked slim. As for standing up to the Silver Arrows and their two lead drivers, Rudi Caracciola for Mercedes and Bernd Rosemeyer for Auto Union, who would be fighting each other at speeds far surpassing anything the Delahaye engine could manage, René believed they stood no chance whatsoever.

CHAPTER 22

On July 25, 1937, almost half a million fans lined the Nürburgring for the German Grand Prix. The very best of the European drivers were there, competing in the fastest of cars. "Make a perfect start—a *perfect* start," Rudi Caracciola repeated to himself from his position in the second row of the grid. Left foot on the clutch, he watched for the signal to go.

On green, he stabbed the pedals and lurched forward, bursting through the first row, past Auto Union's Bernd Rosemeyer, then dove down into the forest. Over the following twenty-two laps, he ran a steady, cold-blooded race.

Rosemeyer was slowed by tire trouble and tried recklessly to recover his lost time. Ernst von Delius and Richard Seaman sparred down a straight at 155 mph and crashed terribly. Others bowed out because of mechanical problems, and Tazio Nuvolari simply could not keep up in his Alfa Romeo. Rudi kept to his plan of two pit stops and a steady pace, and won with a long lead over Manfred von Brauchitsch, followed by Rosemeyer in third. It was a sweet triumph for Rudi over his younger rival.

The next morning, Rudi was flown to Bayreuth, the Bavarian town where the Führer had his country home. Joseph Goebbels, the propaganda minister, was there to welcome him, and then

RUDOLF CARACCIOLA

der erfolgreichste Rennfahrer der Welt

deutscher Meister und Europameister 1935 und 1937

auf

MERCEDES - BENZ

came a round of hearty handshakes with Hitler himself while a photographer took their pictures.

Later, Rudi was paraded through the streets of Stuttgart on the bed of a Mercedes truck that had been covered with flowers. At the gates of Untertürkheim, he was welcomed with a banner that read *Heil dem Sieger* ("Hail to the Victory"), a sea of upraised arms, and his name being chanted to the accompaniment of a brass band. At the party that evening, Wilhelm Kissel handed him a diamond-and-sapphire medallion fixed with a Mercedes star.

Rudi followed his German victory with wins at the Spanish and Italian Grands Prix, where he continued to drive the superb W125 with a mix of aggression, focus, and seasoned experience. At the end of the season, he was named European Champion, toppling Rosemeyer from his throne.

For four years running, the Silver Arrows had monopolized the Grand Prix, fulfilling one of the promises Hitler made at the 1933 Berlin Motor Show. Production figures at Mercedes and other manufacturers were growing by double digits every year, exports were rising, and profits were fat.

The national autobahn project was making huge strides. Hundreds of thousands of workers, fleets of trucks and machinery, tons of iron and steel, and enough concrete to fill 100,000 railroad cars all went into creating 4,287 miles of "Hitler's Highways." The Führer was also moving forward with his dream of putting every German family in their own automobile with the Volkswagen ("people's car"), a project spearheaded by Ferdinand Porsche. NSKK membership was on the rise.

Victory in the Grand Prix was the pinnacle and the inspiration for all these efforts to motorize Germany, and Rudi was again at its apotheosis, the hero of the new Germany. He was celebrated as "Caracciola, the man without nerves," and his every victory was played out in newsreels. Further stoking the Nazi rhetoric, the Goebbels propaganda machine proclaimed him to be a "frontline" soldier in the "racetrack battle" aided by the "brave, small army of mechanics."

Rudi supported the party by taking part in advertising campaigns, speaking at the annual motor show, and appearing beside Hitler and other high officials at public events and private parties. He was, de facto, a standard-bearer of the Third Reich.

Never did the newsreels depict him limping.

CHAPTER 23

In late July, Lucy Schell and her Écurie Bleue established base camp at Montlhéry. They were staying there until they had "Le Million" in the bag. Lucy wanted René Dreyfus to practice until he knew the course as well as he knew his own bedroom.

As August progressed, reporters flocked to Montlhéry to see who was practicing and who might make the first attempt at the Million Prize. Would it be the fabled house of Bugatti? At the beginning of the decade, they had ruled the Grand Prix. Was this to be their comeback, championed by the dashing Jean-Pierre Wimille? Would Émile Petit, the noted engineer of SEFAC, produce a winner after a string of unfulfilled promises? Might Talbot's Tony Lago, who talked a good game, build off his success at the French Grand Prix and field a contender, perhaps with Louis Chiron as pilot? Or could the Delahaye firm, which had dazzled of late with its revolutionary 135, prove that the old French house was indeed a renewed force in motor racing? The presence of René Dreyfus and American spitfire Lucy Schell at the autodrome showed that they were serious indeed.

Such was the drumbeat of questions, stirred by daily newspaper dispatches. With the French on their annual August holidays, there was plenty of spare time for discussion and prediction. "In bars and cafés, on beaches and golf courses up and down the country, it was a matter of fierce discussion," wrote historian Anthony Blight.

By August 10, Jean François had finished the new engine and installed it in the Delahaye 145 René had been testing. "The engine turned like a siren," René praised. Strong, powerful, and consistent, the race car now approached a maximum speed of 140 mph. Together, René and Jean worked on optimizing its performance at Montlhéry.

The shell of the car René used to practice in was thin, unpainted aluminum that looked like it had been hammered out by a half-blind panel beater. To reduce weight, Jean stripped out its second seat.

At first, the Delahaye engineer disdained any insight into "his car" from the driver. What could René know about the technical side of things? He should just drive the car and report on how the car handled various sections of the course. Then Jean himself would decide what was best to do. This did not sit well with René. In his time driving, he had learned a great deal about how a car worked mechanically, how far and how hard he could push an engine, gearbox, brakes, or suspension system.

One afternoon, when René returned to the pits, Jean criticized him for his timidity on the Ascari bend, the long left-hand turn named after the fiery Italian champion, Antonio Ascari, who was killed there during the 1925 French Grand Prix. René took affront at the accusation that fear was holding him back. That had nothing to do with it. He argued that the Delahaye was incapable of handling the bend at the speed Jean wanted. Its tail would fling off the outside edge, just like Ascari's Alfa Romeo had done.

Jean disagreed.

"It's very simple," René said, rising from the front seat. "Take the car, get in, and you'll see."

Certain in his belief, Jean climbed into the Delahaye. René handed over his goggles, and the engineer was quickly away. He returned from a first lap of the circuit. Unsuccessful. He tried again. Failed. One more time, and he came back. "I can't reach that speed on the Ascari bend," Jean admitted. "It's not possible."

René suggested a few changes, including lightening the car, to make the turn easier. Physics, not nerves, was the issue. When Jean returned the Delahaye with the alterations made, René rounded the bend faster than ever before.

From that day forward, Jean understood that there were some things test beds and calculations neglected to quantify. He needed to trust what René felt when he drove, whether it was a change needed in the gear ratio, carburation, braking, or suspension. With each day of tinkering, they wrested out faster laps, improvements measured in half seconds—and often less.

The circuit allowed these trimmings reluctantly. The many hairpins, sharp bends, right-angle turns, and plunging dips at the Montlhéry course chewed up time. Some corners had to be taken almost at a halt. Powerful brakes were essential, top gear was limited to a few straights, and downshifting was a necessary habit.

The design of the course was not the only problem. Its 12.5 kilometers of track and road were a dozen years old and reliant on a government that had little money for repairs. Protruding seams and unlevel sections bedeviled portions of the banked concrete oval, and the tarred road surface was mottled and cracked along its entire length. In addition, gale-force winds often swept across the plateau on which the course was built. Although the summer months were usually calm, there were many days when gusts hit the cars like a wall.

The Écurie Bleue understood the challenges. Every day, often into the night, they worked to overcome them. René brought down his best lap time to 5 minutes 10 seconds—or an average of 145.2 kph (90.2 mph) over the sixteen laps. This was a dramatic reduction of almost 30 seconds from his fastest lap at the recent French Grand Prix, but it was still too slow to win the prize. Over sixteen laps, he needed an average 5 minutes 7 seconds, and, given the standing start, he had to be even faster when he got going to recover time lost in the first lap.

Lucy knew her team had more preparation to do. The Million Franc prize went to the team with the fastest time over 146.5 kph before the deadline, not the first one to achieve that speed.

Bugatti announced that it would make its attempt on Thursday, August 12. Mechanical trouble forced them to postpone by a few days, but on Saturday, August 14, Jean Bugatti, the son and heir of Le Patron, brought his firm's new formula car—a single-seater Type 59 fitted with a 4.5-liter engine—to Montlhéry.

He planned on attacking the Million within the next

forty-eight hours and had already summoned Jean-Pierre Wimille back to Paris for the attempt. Then, en route from the south of France, Wimille suffered a devastating crash on the road.

News of the accident reached Montlhéry early that afternoon. The shock was severe, inside both the Bugatti and Delahaye camps. Phone calls with the hospital reassured them that Wimille would make a full recovery but that he needed to be kept under observation.

Quickly, Bugatti's thoughts turned back to the Million. His star driver was unfit to drive for at least a week. Team captain Robert Benoist might have to make the attempt instead. Benoist had once won four Grands Prix in a single season before Wimille was even out of school, but now, at forty-two, time had slowed his reflexes and dampened his fire.

On August 18, René was making a very fast practice run, and Delahaye looked like they might be ready for their own attempt, when the gearbox broke—due to René's pushing the 145 too hard. They would be delayed from making any prize run for at least several days.

Jean Bugatti thought his injured driver might recover before then, but the Marseilles doctors wanted to keep him under observation a bit longer. At the earliest, Bugatti now figured, Wimille would be ready only a few days before the deadline. If there was poor weather or mechanical trouble, their chance at the Million would disappear. He also had to consider that his star driver might be incapable of the physical effort required to race for 200 kilometers around the Montlhéry track.

Benoist prepared to go himself. In his first attempt, labeled for the press as a practice trial, he quit after a dozen laps because of strong winds. He did not run a lap faster than 5 minutes 9 seconds and told reporters that Wimille could easily have bested his time. "Ah, if I was ten years younger," he added regretfully.

On August 23, the weather cleared, and the winds calmed. Bugatti was confident in his old champion and notified the press that the attempt would take place. They came with photographers and cameramen to record the prize run.

Benoist was very slow from the standing start. "Hesitant," *L'Auto* described it kindly. He finished the first lap in 5 minutes 26 seconds. This was 19 seconds slower than the mean time per lap he needed to maintain for the prize, and it was a tough deficit from which to claw back. In the second lap, he was again too slow—5 minutes 10 seconds—and his time debt deepened.

The Bugatti camp deflated. Benoist really had to get moving now. He gradually improved his times, handling the many turns and bends with considerable skill. The Bugatti ran flawlessly. Nonetheless, he finished in 1 hour 22 minutes 3.9 seconds, 9 seconds over the baseline target—a lifetime when it came to the Million bid.

In the pits, reporters asked Benoist if he would try again. "It's possible," he said before admitting that he hoped Wimille would recover soon. "He is faster than me."

Newspapers reported that the next attempt would probably be coming from René Dreyfus, who continued to practice every day. The spotlight on "Le Drame du Million" was reaching a blinding intensity, and the hope bloomed that France might actually field a worthy Grand Prix car.

Alfred Neubauer sent his staff to keep an eye on the goings-on at Montlhéry. They noted the speeds the Bugatti and Delahaye formula cars could take in corners and their acceleration down straights. Neubauer was unconcerned that the French would prove any competition once the new season began, but it was best to be sure.

Meanwhile, Rudolf Uhlenhaut and his band of engineers and mechanics labored on their new formula car behind the high walls of Untertürkheim. No expense was spared. That year alone, the racing department cost Daimler-Benz 4.4 million Reichsmarks. Wilhelm Kissel said that he supported the team out of the "national interest." This belied how the Nazi government rewarded the company in many ways to compensate for their money-losing Grand Prix operation.

Tax relief, busted trade unions, and highway construction—all had contributed to a recovery at Daimler-Benz that made it the envy of every other automobile company. Gross profits rose yearly, and production and investment returns were skyrocketing. The massive military rearmament program played a critical role in the company's success as well. Its factories were churning out military equipment. With board member Jakob Werlin able to intervene directly with Adolf Hitler, the company won numerous large-scale government contracts. If—and very likely when—war broke out, the company's directors believed that its fortunes would only improve.

To maintain favor over Auto Union with the Reich government, Kissel knew he had to dominate the new Grand Prix formula as they had the previous one. Given their long experience, there was little doubt at Untertürkheim as to which side of the formula—3-liter supercharged versus 4.5-liter unsupercharged—they would choose. At a meeting on March 23, 1937, they decided on a V12 blown engine. The engineers proposed a chassis design based on their 1937 race car but with the drive shaft angled slightly away from the center line, allowing space for the driver to sit even lower to the ground. Wind-tunnel tests on prototype bodies led to improvements in the car's aerodynamics.

After four months of development, these ideas were transformed into finalized plans, and the Daimler-Benz board greenlit production of a minimum of fifteen of the new model: the W154.

CHAPTER 24

Monsieur Charles and Jean François believed that Delahaye and Écurie Bleue were fully prepared for an attempt at the Million. Lucy would have had them try already—she was never one for patience. It was René who remained unsure.

On August 26, he spent hours at Montlhéry, practicing. The broken gearbox had been an easy fix, and the 145 was running very well. To increase its speed, the mechanics had lightened its weight by hollowing out any parts that did not affect its structural integrity. They even punched holes in the gas, brake, and clutch pedals.

At this point, there was little else they could do to the car. Responsibility for the prize now fell on René, and he knew it. He had lost count of how many times he had lapped the course, looking for ways to shave off seconds. Many hundreds—probably more. The cockpit felt as comfortable to him now as an old armchair. He knew every bend and hairpin, every hollow and bump, every landmark that signaled to him where he would soon be. He knew how fast to take each section, where to brake, when to shift, how wide to drift into a turn, at what point to exit it. He knew the angle to enter the autodrome from the road, the height to follow along its banked curve, and the gear to use when shooting through the opening back onto the road circuit.

Still, he felt unready. The offside rear wheel rose slightly from the pavement when he accelerated too much into certain turns. This was costing him time. To avoid this, he needed to know exactly the point at which to stop accelerating in each turn. Most important, he was yet to consistently beat the threshold of 5 minutes 7 seconds.

"You must try tomorrow," Monsieur Charles urged. The weather looked fine. There was very little wind expected. Jean-Pierre Wimille was flying back from Marseille—in fighting shape, or so he was telling reporters. He might make an attempt as early as Saturday. If he was first to break the 146.5 kph average, the pressure on René would only increase. They might even find themselves in a pitched battle to establish the fastest time before the August 31 deadline.

"Dreyfus, I trust you," Monsieur Charles said. "You will go, and you will succeed." As much as he respected Weiffenbach's opinion, René wanted more practice. He did not want to try and fail. "No, I can't do it," he said. "I'm losing too much in the early laps."

"No, you're not."

"Yes, I am."

Monsieur Charles looked at him. He had always told him that the decision to go rested with René and with René alone. "All right. *Bonne nuit.*"

That night, back at their apartment on the western edge of Paris, René and Chou-Chou had dinner together, then took their dog for a walk. They watched the sky darken over the treetops of the Bois de Boulogne. Some time after 10 p.m., they readied for

René on the Montlhéry road circuit during the Million Franc run in August 1937.

bed. Chou-Chou was already in her pajamas when the phone rang. She quickly answered it and spoke in whispers.

After a few moments, René asked. "Who is it?"

"Monsieur Charles," Chou-Chou said before drawing away again.

"What is it about?" René asked, hovering.

"Oh, nothing at all."

"If it's about doing the Million tomorrow, I'm not going."

She waved him away and talked some more to the Delahaye boss. Finally, she hung up and returned to the bedroom.

"What did he want?" René asked, exasperated.

"Oh, nothing!" Chou-Chou said. "He just wanted to know your impressions from your practice earlier. That's all."

Exhausted, René went to bed. His plan for the next day was to start with a long lie-in, followed by an afternoon of practice at the track.

In what felt like mere moments after he had fallen asleep, the alarm clock on his bedside table clattered. It was only 5:30 a.m. He turned to Chou-Chou and grumbled, "There are no tests this morning." He could not understand why she had set the alarm.

"It's all ready," she said, rising from bed. "Come on and get up, René. You're trying the Million today at ten o'clock."

René shook his head. No. No way. Chou-Chou told him that he would never be completely prepared and that he would have to try anyway. She was wrong, René said. He would reach a point when he was sure he could do it. He just needed more time.

Monsieur Charles and Lucy believed differently, Chou-Chou said. They were both convinced that he must shoot for the prize today. Hence the phone call late the night before. They did not want to give him the opportunity to back out.

"No!" René blustered.

"Shut up, calm down, and get dressed," Chou-Chou snapped. The timekeepers were on their way to the track. The press had been informed. As would be everybody in Paris once the morning's papers hit the newsstands, since each would carry news of his scheduled attempt.

René was deeply cross over the deception by his wife and race team. He suspected that his anger had been stirred on purpose by Lucy and Monsieur Charles to make him more aggressive during the run. The thought that he could be played so easily only upset him further.

Shortly after, he drove out of Paris in his black Delahaye coupé, Chou-Chou sitting beside him and their little dog on the back seat. Once off the highway, they rumbled up a rough road toward the plateau where Montlhéry stood. René parked and changed into his white racing suit. When he emerged in the autodrome, he found a crowd of journalists and timekeepers on the track. Still furious, he avoided greeting Monsieur Charles or Lucy.

The Delahaye 145 was ready in the pits, its engine already warmed up. Jean François and his crew had worked overnight to ensure that everything was tip-top with the car, but he wanted René to round a few laps of the course first.

René took his time. It was a gray morning. The pavement was dry. Occasional gusts of wind swept across the plateau, and he knew that any headwind would slow him down. If given the choice, he would have delayed the run. But the decision was no longer his to make. Everybody was on hand and eager that he go.

After a break in the pits, René performed his ritual check of the triple knot on his shoelaces, then climbed back into the cockpit. Everyone was in position, including Chou-Chou, in the timekeeper's stand by the starting line. She would relay his lap times by telephone to a Delahaye mechanic stationed in a water tower a kilometer (.6 mile) into the course. That way, René would know almost immediately how he had done on the previous lap and whether he needed to go faster.

Monsieur Charles came up beside the 145. "You have our confidence," he said. René barely nodded in reply.

A herd of French and foreign journalists, and even a cameraman, were on hand to record René's attempt. Leaning against the wall of the track was Robert Benoist as well.

René placed his hand on the gearshift and readied his feet on the clutch and accelerator. The V12 engine reverberated through to his grip on the steering wheel. The weight of everybody's expectations fell heavy on him. So too did his desire to prove that he had reawakened the fearless instinct that saw him first claim Grand Prix victory. That he deserved to be fielded against the best drivers in the world, regardless of politics, religion, or race.

Sixteen laps. Two hundred kilometers. In 1 hour 21 minutes 54 seconds or less. Every second counted, particularly in the first lap, which was begun from a standing position.

The starter raised the flag. René revved the engine, its guttural rasp breaking through the quiet morning air. His blood felt frozen in his veins. Then the flag dropped, and the Delahaye 145 leaped forward, its tires smoking on the concrete track. René swept past the grandstand and dove off the bowl through a narrow opening onto the tarred road that led from the autodrome.

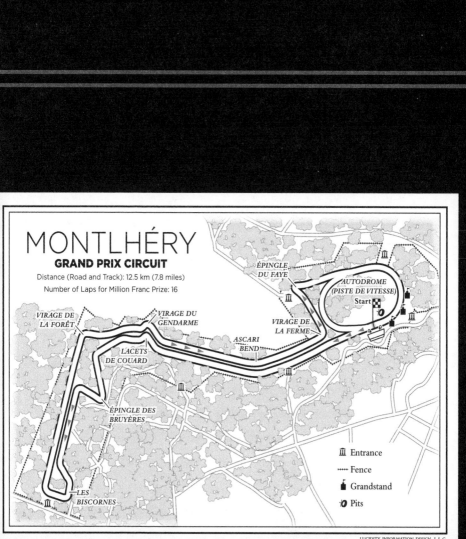

Map of the Montlhéry race course.

CHAPTER 25

It hadn't been the quickest start, and René's arms felt weighted by nerves. He shifted into top gear to take the downhill 2-kilometer (1.25-mile) straight at top speed. To his left was a scattering of trees. To his right, a slender ribbon of grass and wildflowers. At the end of the straight, which he took at almost 140 mph, the road drifted to the right before reaching the Lacets de Couard. The easy part of the course was over.

He rapidly shifted gears through three bends, then the road pitched downward at a steep downgrade into Épingle des Bruyères, a hairpin that had to be taken at a creeping pace. Shortly after that, he crossed the 4-kilometer (2.5-mile) marker and braked as he entered another turn. He could hit fourth gear only briefly in the straight that followed before Les Biscornes, the westernmost point of the circuit. When he emerged from its series of right-hand bends—it resembled a square—he was halfway through the course.

His driving was a little rigid. He worried that he had lost too much time. But there was no way yet to tell. Another kilometer straight followed. It had an uphill grade and could have been taken at top speed throughout except that it was interrupted by a troublesome dip that would have shot his car skyward had he tried. Gusts of wind struck the side of his Delahaye, bucking it slightly off his line.

Just past the 7-kilometer (4.35-mile) marker, the road rose steeply again into the Virage de la Forêt, a right-angle corner by a stand of trees. Shifting out of it, René darted through two gentle bends, making sure to keep his tail from sliding out sideways because of his speed. The course was now generally at an even grade, but his arms and legs got little rest as he was suddenly into another sharp corner.

When he straightened again, René followed the road that ran parallel to the outward-bound stretch of the circuit. Once more he hit top speed.

After the ninth kilometer (sixth mile), he made the long left-hand bend where Antonio Ascari had flipped over and died. René survived the sweep into the straight that followed. Ahead rose the columns of the banked autodrome. He reached the sharp Virage de la Ferme, then tracked the edge of the bowl before braking at the Épingle du Faye, another hairpin.

Desperate to know his time, René barreled through the slender opening back onto the wide concrete surface of the autodrome. He was now opposite the straight on which he had started and almost finished with the first lap. He took the eastern banking of the bowl very fast, centrifugal force keeping his tires on the concrete. Out of the bend, he dove into the straight by the grandstand, making sure to correct from any swerve caused by where the banking met the flat. One lap down. Fifteen to go.

Chou-Chou clicked her stopwatch to register René's time. Onlookers cheered as he passed, their voices lost in the snarl from the 145 engine. Soon after, René looked for his time on the blackboard at the water tower. Five minutes 22.9 seconds. Way too slow. He needed to average 5 minutes 7 seconds on each lap.

Even with the standing start, it was a crushingly bad time. He had a nearly sixteen-second deficit from which to recover. He needed to settle down. He needed to trust himself. The 145 was running well. He could do better — much better.

He swung the wheel back and forth through the Lacets de Couard, braked hard at the Épingle des Bruyères, rounded out of Les Biscornes, and sped along the straight before the Virage de la Forêt. After another stretch of the course and two sharp turns, he returned to the autodrome, then slingshotted out of the banked bowl past the grandstands again. Lap 2 done.

He soon received his time at the water tower: 5 minutes 10.2 seconds. Again too slow. He had done nothing at all to chisel at the deficit and had only added to it. Nineteen seconds to make up now. If he failed to hit the necessary average on the third lap, the attempt might well be lost.

He pushed faster into and out of each turn. Started to feel the course better. His reactions quickened. Third lap: 5 minutes 7 seconds. On mark. Average speed: 146.6 kph (91 mph). It was well won, but René had to improve and knock off one second, maybe two, per lap to climb out of the hole he had dug for himself.

Over the next three laps, he managed to average the same: 5 minutes 7 seconds. It was not good enough. Ten rounds of the circuit remained. Now he had to reduce his times almost to 5 minutes 5 seconds on each and every lap. He was already pushing at the edge of his ability — and at that of the Delahaye.

Eking out a couple of seconds over a 12.5-kilometer course was an immense challenge. René was already taking the best line into each hairpin. His speed in the straights, down the hills, and around the long bends approached the limit of what the car could bear and still hold the road. The brakes and tires could be strained only so much. At best, he might shave tenths of seconds out of each lap.

Any error or misjudgment would cost dear time, but worse, it might launch him off the course or over the top edge of the auto-drome. Drivers had died at Montlhéry in similar record attempts. Shortly after René had left Maserati, one of its drivers, Amedeo Ruggeri, had lost control on the Montlhéry bowl during an attempt at the World's Hour Record. His car somersaulted five times before coming to a standstill on the track, and Ruggeri did not survive.

René had to force away such thoughts—and those of his own crashes in the past. He needed to match his course discipline with boldness.

In the seventh lap, the wind picked up. René blazed around the course, eyes trained on the bumps, dips, and turns ahead. The slim windshield barely cut down the rush of air that buffeted his cheeks. The stretches of grass on the roadside passed in brush-strokes of green. As he cycled through the gears, the bark of his engine deafened him.

His body shook as the Delahaye danced over the uneven, bumpy sections of the tarred road. A hard left. Then a straight. Then a stomach-plummeting descent into the hairpin. After coming around the sharp Épingle du Faye, René whipped into the autodrome. His field of vision down the hood tilted on its side as he drove up the bank. Sky to his left. Concrete to his right. Orientation became difficult, and he had the sensation of being a fly clinging to a wall. There was no rail or fence to stop him from soaring over the top, and every depression in the concrete made his car bounce. He stuck tight and then flung down into the straight.

His time on that lap: 5 minutes 5.6 seconds. That was it. Much better. He had won almost 1.5 seconds from his deficit. Now he had to coax even more speed out of every bend. After the eighth lap, the halfway point, he learned that he had done just that, finishing in 5 minutes 5 seconds flat. He was only 15 seconds down from a Million win. His confidence was growing.

Over the next four laps, he fought the bucking and heaving of the wind to manage slightly better than an average of 5 minutes 5 seconds. He was in rhythm, feeling in perfect union with the Delahaye and their assault together on the course. Fewer than 6 seconds remained in the deficit.

In the stands, Lucy and Laury Schell watched the clock closely, willing René to go faster. Down by the pits, Monsieur Charles and Jean François were doing the same. Their car and their driver needed to stay strong through the final four laps.

René threaded through the thirteenth lap, sure that the constant braking and accelerating were wearing his rear tires thin. He knew this was a risk, and a Dunlop representative was stationed on the road course to alert him if he saw one of the rubber treads giving way to canvas, threatening a burst tire. Such an event would be disastrous to his attempt—and maybe even his life. So far, the Dunlop man had given no indication that anything was wrong.

In the fourteenth lap, René blistered through the straights and turns and clocked his best lap yet: 5 minutes 3.9 seconds. He was now less than half a second in the hole. Everybody in the autodrome, most of all Lucy, sensed the possibility of the Million.

René needed only to run slightly better than 5 minutes 7 seconds. He had done so in the past half dozen laps. Journalists scribbled in their notebooks. The cameraman tried to keep his lens trained on the car as it disappeared through the narrow gates back onto the road course. Chou-Chou spoke rapidly into the phone to the water-tower relay to make sure her husband knew how well he was running. The Delahaye boss and his engineer prayed that the engine would hold.

René whipped down the first straight toward the Lacets de Couard, then down to the Épingle des Bruyères. The Dunlop man, Kessa, was frantically waving his hands. *Tire be damned.* René could not hesitate or falter. He finished the fifteenth lap in 5 minutes 4.3 seconds. Not only had he erased his debt, he now had time in the bank.

Given the threat of the tire bursting, he might have done well to ease off, but he refused to think that way. He urged himself to be braver—bolder.

On the next lap, he glanced at the Dunlop rep. Kessa had a look of horror on his face. René passed him quickly but could have sworn he saw the man make the sign of the cross. Onward. Onward. He rounded Les Biscornes, shot up the straight to the Virage de la Forêt, and coursed through the series of bends until the return toward the autodrome. He swept around the bowl again and slung down past the checkered flag by the grandstand.

The timekeepers clocked 5 minutes 4.5 seconds.

It was a triumph. In the best—and hardest—drive of his life, René had qualified for the Million with an average speed of 146.7 kph (91.2 mph) in a time of 1 hour 21 minutes 49.5 seconds—exactly 4.9 seconds under the limit. If nobody bettered his time by August 31, the prize belonged to Écurie Bleue and to Delahaye.

When René came back around the autodrome, a crowd awaited him on the track. He rolled to a stop, pulled his goggles off his eyes, and lifted himself up onto the back of his seat. Soot covered most of his face, which only made his smile seem all the brighter.

Monsieur Charles and François reached him first, congratulating him with bear hugs. The Schells, sons and all, gathered around the car to cheer him. Delahaye mechanics and staff leaped for joy. Finally, Chou-Chou arrived down from the timekeepers' stand to give him a kiss. As she sat on his lap, photographers took dozens of shots for the next day's front pages.

As the realization set in that he had done it, René stood away from the 145 and wept, both in joy and relief. Lucy Schell and the whole Delahaye crew joined him in his tears. The pop of champagne corks followed, flowers were draped around an exhausted driver, and the whole crowd—journalists and all—retreated to La Potinière, the restaurant beside the autodrome, to celebrate.

As the party was in full swing, a report came in that Jean-Pierre Wimille was flying into Paris that very moment and would make his bid for the Million before the deadline—perhaps as early as the next day. René tried to not allow the rumors to dampen his enjoyment of a well-earned drink.

René qualifies for the Million, August 1937 (left to right: Charles Weiffenbach, Chou-Chou René and Jean François)

CHAPTER 26

Wimille arrived at Montlhéry in the early evening of Saturday, August 28, to test drive the 4.5-liter single-seater Bugatti in which he would make his bid. Pale and with a deep cut marring his upper lip, he wore a bandage around his half-shaved head.

But there wasn't the slightest hesitation in his step when he climbed into his car. After a few laps, he came into the pits, complaining of some gremlins in the engine. The mechanics promised everything would be ready for an attempt on Sunday.

Lucy planned on having René and her 145 ready at the autodrome to run again if Bugatti bested their time. Jean François and his mechanics were overhauling the car back at the factory. They replaced the tires, changed the oil, switched out the spark plugs, greased the suspension, and tightened every nut and bolt within reach. They also washed and shined the rough aluminum body, truly an act of kindness for the ugly little machine.

Early on Sunday morning, Lucy drove out to Montlhéry. René and Chou-Chou were there as well. In a bid to hold on to their luck, René wore the same overalls from his prize run and Chou-Chou the same blue-striped shirt and skirt. Lucy noticed that Monsieur Charles and Jean François had also stuck with the same suits and ties they had been wearing on Friday.

Everybody was tense, especially René, who might have to go

out and better his performance. They spent the day waiting for Wimille and the Bugatti team. Hour after hour passed. Their rivals never showed up. Later that evening, the press reported a statement from Jean Bugatti: "Tomorrow morning, at 8 o'clock a.m., an official attempt will be made."

On Monday morning, August 30, another day of waiting began. A sea of reporters was on hand, as well as timekeepers and ACF officials, to oversee the Bugatti attempt. Again, nobody from the firm appeared. This time there was no statement. After sundown, Lucy and her team departed.

For the third and guaranteed final day, Lucy arrived at Montlhéry early. Yet again, everyone wore the same clothes, except Chou-Chou, who had finally had enough of the old racing superstition. René was a wreck. The constant waiting had frayed his nerves, and the lack of sleep left dark bags under his eyes. At 7 a.m., he ran a couple of test laps with the 145, which performed well. The weather was clear and windless—ideal for an attempt. He spent the rest of the time in the pits, sitting in a chair and fretting.

One hour after the next ticked by, and there continued to be no sign of Bugatti. If they didn't show, midnight would see the Million awarded to Delahaye. By the Fonds de Course rules, only a French *manufacturer* could accept the prize, even though it had been Lucy's ambition—not to mention her money—that had seen their effort through.

She did not need to tell the press that, nor did she court the attention of any reporters, despite their irksome habit of assigning leadership of Écurie Bleue to her husband, Laury. She had come to expect such slights, and no doubt they were part of what fueled her ambition. At least Monsieur Charles had been gentleman enough to promise that the prize would be split evenly between her and the firm if they did win.

As lunchtime came and went, Lucy could only guess at their competitor's intentions. "Were Bugatti and Wimille holding cards they had not yet played?" she asked herself. "Suppose the Bugatti turned up at 6 o'clock in the evening. It would not finish its run until 7:15 p.m. The Delahaye could hardly start another run before half past—and the daylight would have begun to fade long before they could complete it."

She and Weiffenbach asked the fund's committee members to allow René to make his own follow-up run. Nothing in the rules forbade this, and the committee agreed that the 145 could start two minutes after Wimille began—if he began at all. The decision caused race enthusiasts to flow into Montlhéry. The Race for the Million might be an actual race after all.

At 4 p.m., Lucy spotted a Bugatti truck, carrying a single-seater car, emerge from the tunnel. They had come at last. The car was unloaded onto the track by a gaggle of blue-coated mechanics. Jean-Pierre Wimille showed soon after.

The two teams greeted each other, and René shook hands with a tight-jawed Jean-Pierre, the mood akin to two boxers bumping gloves before a fight. Jean-Pierre climbed into his car and took off around the road circuit for a test run.

Minutes passed, many more than the lap should have taken,

Bugatti driver Jean-Pierre Wimille.

before he returned to the autodrome. The car was making an awful racket. Something was wrong.

The Delahaye team watched impatiently as a squad of ten Bugatti mechanics circled it. Word came that the rear axle was broken. It was a significant problem, surely unfixable before the midnight deadline. Odds were that the Million was now in hand and that René might not have to run again. He allowed himself a slight smile.

Remarkably, after over an hour of clanging, welding sparks, and feverish activity, Jean Bugatti declared the car fixed and ready for the attempt. With the sun falling toward the horizon, René slotted his body into the 145 and straightened his white linen cap. He had already earned the Million prize, and he was not about to relinquish it to anybody, let alone the cocksure Jean-Pierre Wimille.

René determined to drive even faster than before. The many hours of waiting had left him anxious but also charged up for a fight. He felt a distinct fire in his veins.

Jean-Pierre was ready at the start. The sky was tinged pale pink, and lights were already glowing around the course. It would be almost dark by the time he and René finished their runs, which only made their attempt even more dangerous.

At 6:43 p.m., the Bugatti launched away, its engine screaming into high gear.

René sat in the 145. Thirty seconds passed. A minute. Thirty seconds more. The countdown began: ten-nine-eight-seven—he prepared to go, feet steady on the pedals—six-five-four-three-two-one . . . The chase was on. Mastering his nerves, he sped after Jean-Pierre as if he needed to overtake him rather than simply beat his time over sixteen laps. His line into every bend and turn was pure and fast, his reflexes instantaneous. He rounded the autodrome to finish the first lap, conscious that he had not sighted Jean-Pierre, nor heard the Bugatti engine over his own.

He streaked past the crowded grandstands. Journalists and radio announcers (and much of France and beyond, who were glued to their wireless radios) took note of his time long before he knew it himself: 5 minutes 19.6 seconds. Passing the water tower on his second lap, René eyed the board held aloft by the Delahaye mechanic. He was 3.3 seconds faster than the standing start in his first Million run but less than half a second better than the chalked time of his rival.

René accelerated. Minutes later, he turned the 145 around the banked bowl and passed the pits. There, surrounded by mechanics, he spotted the Bugatti car, motionless. Jean-Pierre was waving his arms, urging the mechanics to hurry.

René knew only that he planned on finishing what he had started. He clocked 5 minutes 8.1 seconds in his second lap, a 2.1-second improvement on four days before. On he drove, up and down the road circuit, tires screeching in the hairpins, swooping around every bend. Seized by the pure joy of going faster and faster, he finished the third lap at an even better pace. If he continued at this rate, he might cut half a minute off his time.

As René sped into his fourth lap, the Bugatti was ready again. "It's too late," Jean-Pierre said, peering into the sky.

"Go!" Bugatti insisted.

At 7:02 p.m., the single-seater sped away. Now Jean-Pierre was the one chasing René. The two whipped around the road circuit. Coming back toward the autodrome on his fifth lap, René caught the acrid scent of burning oil. He knew it must be from the Bugatti, which would have passed seconds before on the parallel outbound road. Something must be wrong.

He advanced into the sixth lap unaware that Wimille had pulled into the pits again, smoke billowing from his exhaust. Oil was leaking from the engine, and there was no more time left in which to repair it. Their attempt was over.

Shifting quickly through his gears around the course's westernmost point, René continued his race. He finished the lap—5 minutes 7 seconds—and pulled up quickly to a stop. Again, Lucy and the Delahaye crew surrounded him. Again, Chou-Chou wrapped herself around his neck. Again, there were cheers and smiles.

Jean-Pierre threaded a path through the melee to shake his hand. "Bravo! The best man has won today," he said.

The triumph dominated front-page news. Praise in speeches and editorials abounded for René, who had "driven like a god." Weiffenbach was heralded as a living testament to tenacity, and François a designer extraordinaire. Again, seldom was mention made of Lucy, despite efforts by René to highlight her role as the "creator of Écurie Bleue." He stated that her contribution to their success was unparalleled. She knew as much in her heart, but the lack of recognition burned, as always, even if it was expected now.

France had a new national hero. To those who knew of the Dreyfus Affair, it must have been surreal to see that name in the headlines again and realize that a race-car driver of the same name had brought the country together.

Even though René's share of the prize was only a quarter of the total sum—Lucy shared her half with him—250,000 francs was almost three times what he would have earned winning the French Grand Prix. The money was insignificant compared to the confidence the win had given him. In his pursuit of the

Million, René had proved to himself at last that he had the necessary killer instinct to be one of the greats.

Lucy was only getting started. Her first goal achieved, she now set her sights on beating the Germans in the arena they had ruled for years.

PART IV

THE DIVINE AVENGER

CHAPTER 27

At the airport outside Frankfurt, near a Zeppelin airship hangar, Rudi Caracciola stepped up onto a wooden platform to access the cockpit of a custom-built Mercedes. Made to break records, the car was based on the W125 chassis but fitted with a V12, 5.6-liter supercharged engine that delivered enormous amounts of power, more than any car ever built by the company. The body, tested for resistance in a wind tunnel, wrapped around the whole vehicle, even its wheels, and looked like a silver tortoise shell flattened low to the ground.

After Rudi slid into the driver's seat, only the top of his head could be seen by the crowd of onlookers, including schoolchildren, who stood outside the boundary fence. NSKK cars patrolled the opposite side of the highway to prevent anyone from moving onto the road.

From the moment he attained power, Adolf Hitler had set about having Germany break automobile records, and he approved investments in both Mercedes and Auto Union to make it happen. With its long ruler-straight stretches, the new autobahn provided a perfect venue for challenging speed records.

Hans Stuck first led these efforts. As early as 1934, he set several world-class records at AVUS in Auto Union's P-Wagen. Rudi followed with numerous records of his own for Mercedes.

In this way, the feud between the two firms, most visible between Rudi and Bernd Rosemeyer, carried on beyond the Grand Prix.

Today, October 25, 1937, was the opening day of *Reich Rekordwoche* ("Reich Record Week"). Rudi's aim was to break the flying-start records for the kilometer and mile that were held by Bernd. The weather was cold for October, the pavement frosted white, and he had some trouble starting his Mercedes.

Newsreel cameramen and photographers captured every moment of his departure south. As he gathered speed, the Mercedes felt like it was rising up at the front. When he hit 245 mph, Rudi realized that wind pressure under the high-gloss shell had lifted the front wheels almost clear from the pavement. He could not see the road ahead over the nose of the Mercedes, and he had lost his ability to steer.

It took every bit of his nerve and skill to slow the car down while keeping it pointed forward. Otherwise, Rudi would surely have flashed off the road, most likely in a terrible series of flips and pirouettes. The attempt abandoned, he returned to the Mercedes pit by the airship hangar and informed Rudolf Uhlenhaut of the issue. His team tried to fix the problem but were unsuccessful, and their hopes for Record Week were dashed.

Bernd was next out in his aerodynamically shelled 16-cylinder P-Wagen. He held the steering wheel with a featherlight touch— adjustments beyond a millimeter or two at such velocities would be catastrophic. Every seam in the road jolted the car and left its chassis vibrating like a tuning fork.

Bernd Rosemeyer in his Auto Union record breaker, October 1937.

Almost every mile, there was a bridge underpass, and when he entered, Bernd felt a punch to the chest from the displaced air. Then, when he exited, a split second later, he needed to counteract the car's violent side swerve. At one point his heart was beating so fast that he was dizzy to the verge of losing consciousness.

Over the next three days, Bernd broke a trio of world records and a dozen world-class records, including long-distance records such as the 10 Mile. He also clocked over 250 mph, achieving his grand ambition and beating Rudi Caracciola to the milestone. The 1937 Reich Record Week was a resounding success, a fact trumpeted by the propaganda ministry at every opportunity.

Neither Rudi nor Mercedes could allow their nemesis's records to stand unanswered for a whole year, and so Kissel and Werlin began pushing Hühnlein to allow another record attempt to take place before the next Berlin Motor Show. Their impatience would ultimately doom one of Germany's greatest-ever drivers and fulfill the warning Bernd had once given Rudi after a particularly heated duel on the track: "We cannot go on this way . . . One of us will die."

Focus on the upcoming Grand Prix season intensified by the day. On the French side, it looked like Louis Chiron might represent Talbot, where Tony Lago was reportedly building a V16 engine. Jean-Pierre Wimille would surely be back with Bugatti. The Italian firms Alfa Romeo and Maserati, long-suffering in defeat, were intent on returning to the victory stands. In March 1937, Alfa Romeo had bought out Enzo Ferrari's Modena operation, although the company allowed him to run the team and its cars largely as he saw fit. Despite the skill of Tazio Nuvolari, they rarely posted any wins outside Italy.

Nuvolari was under political pressure to remain on the team, now renamed Alfa Corse, despite recruitment efforts from Auto Union. The Flying Mantuan was losing patience with such nationalistic demands, especially since the new Alfa formula car, the Tipo 308, was largely a rehash of a former design.

Most attention focused on the Germans. Auto Union's car was reported to be powered by a 3-liter, supercharged V12 engine, now located mid-chassis rather than in the rear. Mercedes was bench-testing a similar type of engine. "Going on past form," *Autocar* stated, echoing the predictions of most, "the German cars are likely to prove superior again."

Shortly before Christmas, Monsieur Charles traveled to Reims to meet delegates from every manufacturer fielding cars in the 1938 season. Neubauer, Costantini, Bugatti, Lago, Maserati—they were all there. Over a lavish dinner in the vaulted cellars of legendary champagne producer Louis Roederer, they finalized the schedule of races. The season opener would be a round-the-houses circuit, but not at Monaco, as was traditional. Instead, the provincial French town of Pau was selected.

At Pau, competitors in the new formula would face off against each other for the first time. Teams would want to demonstrate their cars had what it took to dominate throughout the year. Drivers would aim to show how sharp their skills were—and how intent they were on victory. The race on April 10 would truly be a proving ground.

CHAPTER 28

In Frankfurt, on January 27, 1938, high winds and steady rain postponed all record attempts. The winter date, rammed through by Mercedes to precede the Berlin Motor Show, was always going to be a challenge. The next day before dawn, the winds had settled, and the clouds over Frankfurt cleared.

In the predawn gleam of the pale moonlight, the Mercedes car in which Rudi Caracciola was to make the attempt looked like a spaceship. Uhlenhaut and his engineers had refined the car to provide more stability at high speeds. They also shaped the body to eliminate the lifting action that had nearly killed Rudi the previous October.

At 5 a.m., Rudi and his backup driver, Manfred von Brauchitsch, drove slowly down the autobahn in a regular car, looking for any imperfection in the surface or break in the pine trees where the wind might blow through. After the finish, there was a section of road unprotected by trees that was at risk of dangerous side winds.

Fortunately, the air that morning was almost still, but Rudi was troubled by the frost that covered the pine woods, the highway, and the strip of grass between the opposing carriageways. He insisted they wait until the sun had melted the slick white coating.

By eight o'clock, the frost had disappeared from the road. Dressed in his racing overalls, Rudi headed to the highway where the Mercedes crew had readied his car. He stuffed wax in his ears and climbed inside. The mechanics secured the Plexiglass dome over his head. At 8:20 a.m., the timekeepers were ready, and Neubauer shouted, "Go!"

Mechanics gave the Mercedes a push, and Rudi took off down the autobahn, shifting gears and gathering speed before he reached the timed section. 100 mph. The treble note of the compressor pierced the winter morning. 150 mph. The road ahead narrowed into the slender line of an arrow shaft. 200 mph. The trees on either side of the road fused into a single bordering wall of black.

250 mph.

Rudi crossed the beginning of the timed section, feeling that he was already pushing the Mercedes to its maximum. Moments later, he passed the waving flag at the finish of the mile distance. He dared not apply the brakes. Instead, like letting air gradually out of a balloon, he released the pressure on his accelerator and allowed the car to roll to a stop.

Several mechanics raced over to him and unbolted the dome, and Rudi sucked in fresh air. They shook his hand, their shouting voices muted and tinny after the din of the engine that still echoed in his skull. Then they turned the car around and led it back to the finish line.

Rudi waited for the telephone call reporting his time. He smoked a cigarette, his fingers trembling as the adrenaline

Rudi torpedoes down the highway in his world-record speed run for Mercedes, January 1938.

drained away. "It's a record, Mr. Caracciola!" someone announced. He had completed the mile in 13.42 seconds at a colossal "average" speed of 268.3 mph. Jubilation exploded around him, but he still had to make the run back to the start line. The official record would be his only if the mean average of the two runs was faster than the speed Bernd had posted in October.

He got back in the car and, minutes later, shot forward once again. The car was moving faster than his mind could process his immediate surroundings. He trained his gaze far down the road to anticipate any decisions he would have to make. Aiming the car through the underpasses felt like threading the eye of a moving needle.

Another wave of a flag. Another rush of people. He had bettered his time by four-hundredths of a second. His average speed over the two runs was 268.5 mph. It was a new world-class record.

"You want to do one more?" Neubauer asked. Rudi shook his head, unable to muster words after pushing so close to the brink of death.

Back at the hotel, Rudi was having a late breakfast when he learned that, as expected, Bernd Rosemeyer was on his way to the autobahn to make an attempt. Auto Union wanted to snatch back the record before the next newspaper edition.

Reluctantly, Rudi left to watch the attempt. Although this

second round of record breaking had been at his instigation, he knew these attempts should not be run like races. They were already too dangerous, and the best time of day to make them was early morning, when the wind was at its calmest.

He took a look at the windsock above the airship hangar. It stretched straight out, with occasional gusts to the left. It was madness that Rosemeyer would try to reclaim the record in those conditions. Pushing through the throng, Rudi approached the Auto Union driver.

"Congratulations," Bernd said.

"Thank you," Rudi returned. He should say something about the wind, warn Bernd off the attempt. He stayed silent. He would not have liked anyone raising doubts with him when he was about to drive. At those speeds, nerves could kill.

Off Bernd went with a scream of his engine, and his silver car disappeared around the bend in the road. Half an hour later, he returned in a flash. Over the two runs, he averaged 268 mph for the mile. His second run was much faster than the first, and he and his team thought their chances were good to retake the record on the next try.

At 11:46 a.m., he sped down the autobahn. Nobody knows for certain what happened next, whether a gust hit the side panel of the streamlined car or whether Bernd altered his road position in anticipation of the wind. But something went irreversibly wrong. At over 250 mph, Bernd's tires brushed the grass on the left edge of the road. The car skidded at an angle across the road, an uncontrollable slide. The aerodynamic shell tore away, and

Bernd Rosemeyer at the start of the record attempt that cost his life, January 1938.

the car somersaulted several times in a blur of silver, disassembling as it went.

Bernd was thrown out of the cockpit, and landed in the woods over 80 yards from the road. What was left of the car hobbled to a stop on the embankment. The trail of wreckage was strewn along the highway for over 500 yards. Back at the airport parking lot came the report: "The car has crashed!" The entire Auto Union team who were present, and many others too, hurried out to the site. Two bystanders found Rosemeyer's body resting at an awkward angle against a tree trunk. His face looked serene; his eyes were open.

News reports announced the tragedy to a shocked German public. In his diary, Joseph Goebbels wrote, "A deadly misfortune. Our best driver is lost in a great and completely unnecessary record race."

Goebbels was always one to see and seize an opportunity, and a state funeral was arranged. Wearing white racing overalls, Rudi and several other German drivers led the cortege, with SS officers standing at attention along the route. The many letters of condolence from Nazi high officials were leaked to the press for maximum effect. Hitler sent Elly a telegram, writing that "the news of your husband's tragic fate has left me shaken. May the thought that he fell fighting for Germany's reputation lessen your great grief."

There was little investigation into what caused the accident. No blame was assigned, at least not publicly, to the decision by Auto Union to allow Bernd to make his run—or to attempt to break a speed record in the middle of winter. As Korpsführer Hühnlein wrote to Kissel on December 1, 1937, when initially approving the "chivalrous match," the "exceptional propaganda appeal at home and abroad" was worth the risk.

CHAPTER 29

Three weeks later, on February 18, Rudi led a phalanx of Silver Arrows through the center of Berlin and down the broad tree-lined avenue to the Kaiserdamm for the launch of the Berlin Motor Show. Twenty thousand NSKK troops lined their path, and behind them, crowds of Berliners watched and waved. At the end of the long procession of motorcycles and cars, Adolf Hitler and his chief officials traveled in a line of limousines.

Outside the exhibition hall, the drivers revved their engines, the yelp of their superchargers deafening the crowd. Hitler loved it and offered handshakes and other pleasantries to his racing champions before stepping into the entrance hall. Trumpets sounded as he walked up to a platform set in front of swastika flags that rose nearly as high as the glass rooftop.

In his speech, Hitler spoke about his "beloved child": the automobile industry; the NSKK's success in training 150,000 young men to drive; the thousands of miles of the autobahn that had been built; and the huge plant soon to be built to produce the "People's Car." Then he declared the exhibition open. Behind him, curtains were swept aside to reveal the main hall and the displays of cars, among them the streamlined Mercedes in which Rudi had broken his world speed records.

Two days later, Hitler delivered another speech, this one in the Reichstag, stating that "over ten million Germans live in two of the states adjoining our border." In his view, it was unbearable that they did not enjoy his protection. He was being far from coy. Seven million German-speaking people lived in Austria; three million Sudeten Germans lived in Czechoslovakia; and he had just put the world on notice that they belonged to the greater Reich.

He now waited for his opportunity to unite Germany and Austria. Nazi mobs took over the streets and town halls in Austria, and German tanks, motorized columns, and airplanes swept into the country on March 12. Hitler followed in an open-topped gray Mercedes, stopping at his birthplace of Braunau am Inn, then at his childhood home of Linz. Church bells rang, and the crowds waved swastika flags and cheered the arrival of their conquering hero, who stood ramrod straight in the front seat, one hand on the windshield, the other raised in salute. He then journeyed to Vienna to seal the union (*Anschluss*) of the two countries. As one of his ministers stated, Hitler was in "a state of ecstasy."

Spasms of violence overtook the capital, most of it directed at the Jewish community. Mobs threw bricks through the windows of Jewish shops and looted their owners' wares. "Individual Jews were robbed on the open streets of their money, jewelry, and fur coats," historian Ian Kershaw wrote. "Groups of Jews, men and women, young and old, were dragged from offices, shops, or homes and forced to scrub the pavements in 'cleaning squads,' their tormentors standing over them and watched by crowds of

Jews forced to clean the streets after the *Anschluss* of Austria.

onlookers screaming 'Work for the Jews at last,' kicking them, drenching them with cold, dirty water, and subjecting them to every conceivable form of merciless humiliation."

Nobody, whether in Europe or in the United States, lifted a finger to stop Hitler from annexing Austria or to prevent the violence that ensued in the streets. In the House of Commons,

Neville Chamberlain said, "The hard fact is that nothing could have arrested what has actually happened—unless this country and other countries had been prepared to use force." American journalist William L. Shirer wrote plainly in his diary: "Britain and France have retreated one step more before the rising Nazi power." After returning to Berlin, Hitler announced that a vote would be held in Germany and Austria to sanction the union between the two countries. He scheduled the vote for April 10, the same day as the opening of the Grand Prix season at Pau.

Songbirds trilled in the trees, and a rabbit hopped across the grass. The rising sun evaporated the last of the dew. In the distance, a shrill note rose over the landscape. The birds grew silent. The rabbit hunkered down. The sound grew quickly, swelling with intensity and penetrating the air with a raspy growl.

All of a sudden, a silver Mercedes, its hood removed to allow easy access to its engine, swept over a rise into view, Rudi Caracciola at the wheel. He pointed the ground-hugging Arrow through a chicane and then vanished almost as quickly as he had come. Only the wail of his 3-liter supercharged engine—which a reporter likened to the cry of "ten thousand scalded cats"— remained, before that too faded away.

The V12 engine was finished in early January and had received its first test in the workshop at Untertürkheim and on the autobahn. But nothing would give the engineers a better idea about the state of the car—and what needed refining—than these trials at the Monza track, just outside Milan.

The circuit provided a range of hairpins, curves, straights, and changes in elevation, and when it failed to provide the exact conditions they wanted, they set up pylon barriers to create chicanes, tighten corners, and shorten straights. Uhlenhaut and Neubauer even created a mocked-up course to simulate the Pau Grand Prix circuit. Every day, they drove the car hundreds of miles, often to breaking point.

Neubauer and Uhlenhaut ran the operation like scientists, isolating variables in a series of controlled experiments. They tested tire wear, the brakes, how the car held to the road, and fuel consumption, and noted everything in daily reports. It was an expensive, time-consuming operation, supervised by numerous mechanics who burned through fuel, tires, and patience. But the car was running well. It was running very well.

CHAPTER 30

On Thursday, April 7, two Delahaye trucks, painted on their sides with the bulldog mascot and the name Écurie Bleue, advanced through southwestern France. René Dreyfus and his fellow team driver, Gianfranco "Franco" Comotti, formerly of Ferrari, followed in their own coupés.

Lucy Schell would not be joining the Delahaye team in Pau — she had arranged to compete in a Concours d'Élégance in Cannes at the same time. She had done everything in her power to make sure the Delahaye 145 and René had their best shot at coming out on top. In money alone, she had spent over 2 million francs to support the design of the 145, win the Million, and prepare for the 1938 season.

Neither Lucy nor René recorded their last conversation in person before the race. One can imagine she invited him to her home in Brunoy, where she liked to meet her drivers, to be sure of their full attention. The German annexation of Austria and the bloody violence in the streets of Vienna were dominating the news. Perhaps over tea in her drawing room overlooking the Yerres River, she told René that a victory at Pau would not change the tides of nations, but that a win over the Silver Arrows would spark hope in a world darkening at every turn.

She had launched her team to hit back against the Nazis'

march toward dominance in every field. As Jewish American Max Baer said before his knockout fight against Max Schmeling, "Every blow to Schmeling's eyes is a blow against Hitler." Lucy may have said all of this or nothing, but what is certain is that for the first time in his career, René left for a race understanding that there was more at stake than who crossed the finish line first. By winning, he would make a statement about his being excluded from German and Italian teams because of his Jewish heritage.

He had heard too much about what the Nazis were doing in Germany and now Austria. He despised their actions and feared what they might do next. He understood that while he did not identify as Jewish himself, this was of little importance. Many people saw him that way—those rooting for him, and those against him. He would never fully outrun his name. Any blow he could strike against the Nazis' theories of their own superiority was a blow he wanted to make, and if he won at Pau, his victory would be a symbolic triumph against Nazi thuggery.

Years before, in words that had stuck with René for the rest of his life, Meo Costantini had told him that he needed to be more aggressive. In his run for the Million, René had transcended that advice. Now the rest of Costantini's words came to mind: If he truly wanted to become a great driver, he needed to "find something to struggle and fight for."

As he drove toward Pau, René knew that he had found that something.

In the late afternoon, he sighted Pau up ahead. The small city stood in the distance like a serene jewel. Set on a plateau overlooking the Gave de Pau River, Pau had medieval charm and a remarkable setting. In the nineteenth century, wealthy visitors from across Europe, Russia, and the United States poured in, and grand mansions—and even grander hotels—were established. Spas, casinos, and theaters followed. A long promenade shaded by plane trees was built on the edge of the plateau as well as a funicular to connect the aptly named Boulevard des Pyrenees to the bustling train station beside the river below.

As Écurie Bleue arrived in the town, the streets were alive with preparations. Near the start, a line of six covered grandstands was being readied, PA systems tested, and the competitor leaderboard positioned.

René and Franco Comotti helped Jean François and his mechanics unload the 145s. The Écurie Bleue had few spare hands and was a shoestring operation, especially when compared to Mercedes, whose ranks arrived that same day in a convoy of five large trucks, like an invading army, Alfred Neubauer their commanding general.

Mercedes had three drivers for their two cars, reserve engines for both vehicles, and enough equipment to build a whole other car from scratch. Beyond a battalion of engineers and mechanics, the team also brought a doctor, tire and fuel experts from Continental and Shell, and several hack journalists to provide a supply of pro-German stories to the press back home.

CHAPTER 31

The next morning, a clear, sunny day, René left his hotel, a grand old establishment on the Place Royale whose rooms looked out on the snow-capped peaks of the Pyrenees, and took the funicular down to the pits, where his Delahaye 145 was fueled and ready. Its body had been painted blue with stripes of red and white that began at the nose of the hood and ran down either side of the car. On each door was painted the number 2, René's number in the race. Comotti's car was painted with a 4, but otherwise his 145 was almost indistinguishable from that of his team leader.

The Delahayes drew only a fraction of the attention given to the Mercedes W154s. This was the first public appearance of the new model, and drivers Rudi Caracciola and Hermann Lang had to wade through journalists and photographers to reach their vehicles.

Fulfilling the ambitions of the new formula, the competitors also presented a range of designs and engine sizes. Jean-Pierre Wimille was on the roster for the Bugatti team, reportedly with a new 3-liter supercharged car. Three independent drivers, including Maurice Trintignant in his first Grand Prix race, were also piloting Bugattis, but older models. René Le Bègue, two-time winner of the Monte Carlo Rally, and another driver had entered the same type of Talbot that Louis Chiron had driven to win the

1937 French Grand Prix. With the two Écurie Bleue Delahaye 145s and an independently driven 135, that was the sum of the French-built cars.

The field of sixteen promised a very fine race, over one hundred grueling laps. The winner would earn a 30,000-franc prize, but more important, the prestige of claiming the first victory of the new formula. Before the practice sessions had even taken place, Caracciola and Nuvolari ranked as the clear favorites.

After a few spins around the course, Nuvolari shot off under the noon sun for the first timed trial. He delivered on his devil-may-care reputation, whipping his Alfa Romeo Tipo 308 around the course in 1 minute 48 seconds and beating his own lap record, set at the 1935 Pau Grand Prix. It was an impressive run, and the Italian champion flashed a toothy grin to the photographers and cameramen in the pits.

René performed well too. Feeling confident from the start, he posted a 1:50 lap, just behind Nuvolari. Lang finished third in his W154, with 1:51, then Caracciola with 1:53, followed by Alfa Corse's Emilio Villoresi, at 1:56, and Comotti in the other Delahaye at 2:01.

Nuvolari decided to see if Villoresi's single-seater performed better than his own. Again, he took off sharply from the start, drove around the turn by the funicular, and up the Avenue Léon Say, climbing alongside the arched stone viaduct that supported the promenade above. After several more turns, he reached Parc Beaumont on the plateau.

A spectator noticed a trail of liquid on the road after Nuvolari sped by and thought it might be gasoline. Others saw it as well, and a call was made to issue a stop signal on the circuit. By the time one came, it was too late.

Before Nuvolari realized the danger, his Tipo was already wrapped in flames. He had been going at such a speed that he did not see the fire for several seconds, and he reacted only when the heat reached his legs. To wait until the car stopped would mean burning alive. There was only one other option. Moving at 25 mph, he pushed himself up out of the cockpit and threw himself onto the road. Flames licked his clothes as he rolled on the pavement, unconscious from the fall. Two French students rushed over to beat the flames away.

The unmanned Tipo 308, now a rolling ball of fire, careered off the course into a hedge opposite a lake. By the time emergency crews could be marshaled, the blaze had consumed the car.

An ambulance carried Nuvolari to the hospital, where the doctors and nurses treated the second-degree burns to his arms, legs, and back, as well as facial abrasions caused by his leap out of the car. During a visit to his hospital bed, Rudi jokingly asked why his former teammate had not directed "the car into the lake just to cool it off." Nuvolari was in no mood for humor.

The fuel tank of his Tipo 308 had ruptured in one of the turns because the chassis had too much flex in it. Already unhappy with Alfa Corse and the state of its cars, he decided to retire from the team, effective immediately. Fearing that the same problem might afflict all the Tipo 308s, the other Italians backed out of the race as well.

The field had already thinned that day. Jean-Pierre Wimille never showed up—the new Bugatti wasn't ready—and Talbot clocked such poor runs in the practice rounds that they decided to scratch themselves from the roster. With the withdrawal of Nuvolari, Rudi was an even surer bet among the ten remaining competitors. Such was the confidence of the Mercedes team that they went sightseeing in nearby Lourdes.

The next day, Saturday, the crowds gathering in Pau enjoyed another fine, cloudless afternoon for the second set of timed trials. Rudi got a better jump at the start, but René followed close behind, maintaining contact throughout the course while also studying the best lines to take in every turn.

Coming out of some of the corners, he noticed the rear wheels of the W154 overspinning. He sensed that this was something he could use to his advantage.

Rudi finished the second session with the fastest time, 1:48. Lang matched this, though he suffered a minor crash and experienced engine trouble. Neubauer logged every lap time, along with every issue his drivers reported in specific turns, in a black notebook. He also oversaw every tire change and refueling.

Uhlenhaut and his team took enough temperature readings to make a meteorologist blush, as they were aware that the heat had an effect on the engine, tire pressure, and state of the road. They analyzed the brakes, tread wear, and fuel consumption; they even drained some of the oil to be tested later in their mobile lab. Throughout the trials, they adjusted the gear ratios to find the right balance between top speeds and maximum acceleration out of the many corners on the short, winding course. Uhlenhaut had yet to solve the overspinning of the rear wheels. A German victory was not just expected: It was required. Nothing could be left to chance.

Neubauer also kept a hawk eye on the competition. René Dreyfus posted a best lap time only two-tenths of a second behind the two W154s. Comotti clocked the fourth best at 1:59, then came Dioscoride Lanza in his Maserati at 2:00.

In Stuttgart, Wilhelm Kissel waded through the reams of reports that were being relayed by telephone from his racing team in Pau. Nuvolari was definitely out. "This takes away our most dangerous opponent," read one dispatch. "But the Grand Prix is far from being decided in our favor. In today's training, Dreyfus for Delahaye was able to stay close to Caracciola." With the loss of so many competitors, Pau looked to be "a fight only between Mercedes-Benz and Delahaye."

The German team had other concerns. Dreyfus would likely not need to refuel, while the Mercedes drivers would. Their 3-liter supercharged engine gobbled up the noxious WW fuel at a rate of 1.6 miles per gallon. Also, the high temperatures at Pau made the asphalt spongy and slick, causing excessive tire spin. Finally, Uhlenhaut needed to replace the engine on Lang's car. The oil pump was faulty, and the spark plugs continued to get mucked up during practice. They would work overnight to make the switch. Despite these issues, the reports stated, Caracciola and Lang were pleased with the W154s. *Flawless* was the term they used. There was every reason to believe they would win.

In this opinion, the drivers were well supported. Over the past week, the Daimler-Benz press department had pumped out press releases highlighting the "mastery of German engineers" and the supremacy of Rudi Caracciola. Scores of newspapers parroted the same and forecast a likely win by the Silver Arrows in the opening race of the new formula. After all, neither a French driver nor a French car had managed to beat the Germans in any Grand Prix event since Hitler first funded their racing teams. Even the patriotic French publication *L'Auto* begrudgingly predicted, "Surely, Mercedes should win."

One newspaper best summed up the forecasts for Pau: "The outcome of this race is now such a complete certainty that no bookmaker would take any money on the Germans, even at heavy odds-on prices. The Germans don't make the kind of mistakes peculiar to the average mortal, and with Caracciola and Lang driving, what is there to add?"

Wilhelm Kissel was depending on a win at Pau, especially since it was being held on the same date as the plebiscite vote on the *Anschluss*. Hitler had barnstormed Germany and Austria to rally support for what was already a foregone conclusion. His propaganda ministry made sure the ballot was printed with a huge circle to mark *Ja* and a punch-hole-size circle for *Nein*.

Kissel had done his own campaigning in support of the referendum. He tied the success of Mercedes and its racing team to his "beloved leader" and reasoned that Austria, "our brother," should return to the family to benefit from the same. "Hitler brought the German automobile industry from the edge of the abyss with a strong hand and paved the way for its unprecedented rise," Kissel said in one of his speeches. "For this we must thank him—whether worker, engineer, salesman, technician, or director—on April 10, 1938 with all our hearts through our 'Yes!'"

In a final speech, Kissel remarked that "victory in the Grand Prix was not only a victory of the driver and builder in question, but always at the same time one of the whole nation." Defeat at Pau would be a humiliation.

At the end of the day, the drivers left their cars in the pits and returned to their hotels to bathe away the oil stains and gasoline fumes. The mechanics piloted the cars back to their garages—in neck-jerking low gear—to be wiped down and prepared for the next day. The starting grid was set, and the sun went down on a city eager for the battle ahead.

CHAPTER 32

René Dreyfus paced his room at the Hotel de France, his mind churning. Since becoming a Grand Prix driver, he had not beaten Rudi Caracciola in a single race. Compared to the Delahaye, Rudi's W154 was faster off the line, produced almost double the horsepower, and benefited from far more advanced brakes and suspension. From Alfred Neubauer down to the mechanics, Mercedes boasted a professional operation that was exhaustive in its preparations and lightning quick in the pits.

Nonetheless, René had spotted three weaknesses during the timed trials that would play well in his favor. First, the Mercedes cars would need to refuel midrace while he would not. The Delahaye had a large gas tank and burned fuel much more economically. Second, the W154s often suffered from wheel spin in the corners because their engines were so powerful. Too much throttle, and Rudi and Hermann Lang would lose traction—and time—throughout the course. In contrast, the Delahaye hugged the pavement coming out of turns.

Third, René had never shifted out of third gear on even the longest straight on the course. It was simply too short to gather much speed. One hundred miles an hour was probably the maximum one could take it at. This meant that the W154s would be unable to use speed to their full advantage.

René boiled down these observations into a clear, simple strategy: Stay tight with Rudi and Hermann; never allow them to gain too much distance; and finally, when they need to refuel, seize the lead and never give it back.

By winning the Million, René had proved to himself that he could run an aggressively disciplined attack and that his Delahaye was equal to the task. But Pau was a real race, run over one hundred laps through the city on a narrow course, where he would have to struggle against other competitors. A single mistake entering a turn, a single mechanical failure, a single stroke of bad luck could ruin his chances at victory—or worse.

Unlike in the Million, there would be no returning to the start to have another go. Not since his first Grand Prix victory at Monaco in 1930 had René wanted to win more. Then he had chased the checkered flag solely for himself. The world had changed, and so had he, and now there was much more to fight for.

The rising sun cast the Pyrenees in hues of gold and pink, and across the cobblestone streets of Pau the scent of freshly baked baguettes wafted from boulangeries, and espresso machines gurgled and hissed in cafés. The caretaker of the Château de Pau swept the steps with a grass broom, the swish-swish-swish as lulling as the tick of a clock.

Slowly, with a gathering momentum, the city awakened, and a steady flow of cars and pedestrians converged on its center. Spectators who wanted a particularly good view lined up early in the morning, and by noon roughly 50,000 people packed the grandstands and ticketed areas around the course. It was a fraction of the number that attended the Nürburgring, but the much shorter course of Pau meant that the density of the crowd was similar. The heat had broken since the practice sessions, and they could not have had a more beautiful, cloudless blue day.

That morning, while the other teams focused solely on the competition ahead, thirty-four members of the Mercedes team, including the drivers, gathered in their hotel to vote in the referendum. To the question—"Are you in agreement with the reunion of Austria with the German Reich as effected on March 13?"—they unanimously responded, "Ja!" A Mercedes official forwarded their tally to Untertürkheim by telephone. The team, some of whom had already labored overnight to install the reserve engine in Lang's car, then went back to work.

The pits hummed with activity. Crews inspected their cars, which they had driven down from their overnight garages. They stacked towers of tires, rolled out drums of fuel, rigged their force-feed lines, and set out toolboxes—all before the drivers arrived.

In his room at the Hotel de France, René took off his wedding ring and wristwatch, leaving them on his bedstand to collect after the race. Their removal was an acknowledgment that he might well die that day. He triple-knotted his shoes and clipped off the ends of the laces to prevent a snag on a pedal. Then it was time to go.

From the original sixteen, the field had been cut in half. Both Nuvolari and Lang had dropped out (Lang because of trouble with his oil pump). None of the other drivers had approached their lap times in practice. To the organizers, this was a disaster, but to many others, it created the possibility of an epic duel:

Dreyfus versus Caracciola.
Delahaye versus Mercedes.
France versus Germany.

At last, all the drivers were on the scene. Autograph seekers shouted for attention and waved their red-and-white race programs. There would be time for that after the race. In the Delahaye pit, Jean François reconfirmed with René their strategy: Stick to Rudi Caracciola until he needed to refuel, take the lead, and never give an inch back on it.

Rudi had no need to go over strategy with Neubauer. He intended to shoot off like a rocket from the start and gain an unassailable gap from Dreyfus, regardless of the need to refuel at the midway point.

As 2 p.m. approached, the mechanics pushed the cars out of the pits to the strains of a traditional Pau tune played by a band of trumpeters. They manuevered toward the grid, located roughly a hundred yards in front of the grandstands, where white marks on the pavement indicated where the cars should stand. Rudi's Mercedes was on the left of the front row, René's Delahaye to its right. Staggered behind them in three rows were the rest of the competitors.

Charles Faroux, dressed in a summer suit and hat, called the

The start of the 1938 Pau Grand Prix.

eight drivers together in a circle to advise them on the rules. After the briefing, the drivers milled about the pits. Their crews tried to distract them with small talk, but it was pointless. Now that they were approaching zero hour, there was little to think about apart from the race. Some of the drivers adjusted, then readjusted, their gloves or wiped their goggles for the tenth time. No one stood still.

"Five minutes," Faroux shouted. "To your cars."

Rudi limped across to his Mercedes. His gait had been uneven

since his accident at Monaco five years before. Around his neck and tucked neatly into the top of his overalls he wore a polka-dotted scarf to protect from the dust.

Wearing sunglasses against the glaring sun, René headed to his Delahaye, polishing a new pair of goggles as he walked—he never wore the same pair twice. He fitted his cap over his head, slipped on his tan leather gloves, then pulled the goggles over the top of his head.

In the grandstands, the loudspeakers silenced, and a hush fell over the crowd, now all on their feet, gazing at the cars, waiting . . . waiting . . .

On the grid, René eyed Rudi. The German driver returned the look. The other drivers shared their own glances: some grinning, others stone-faced. Then, like a thunderclap, one car roared into life. Then two. Then all eight. The air seemed to shudder, and the clamorous beat of the engines took on a rhythm of its own in the chests of everyone close by. The drivers tapped on their throttles, quickening the beat, as the track cleared of mechanics and officials. The air thickened with exhaust whose "various dopes," one reporter wrote, "suggested boot polish and tinned pineapple."

Rudi rechecked his gear level, his tachometer, his foot pedals, his rearview mirrors. All fine, he rubbed the side of his leg, knowing well the pain that would come with a hundred laps of the winding circuit.

René sat upright in the cockpit, straight and tense as a board. He trained his gaze on Faroux.

Standing on the front right edge of the grid, the race director turned his wrist to read his watch. It was time. He held the French tricolor flag aloft in one hand and raised the other to count down the seconds.

René tightened his grip on the gearshift and revved his engine. The Delahaye throbbed around him, and the cacophony sounded like the final movement of a stirring symphony.

As the crowd swayed forward, necks craned toward the start, Faroux whipped down the flag.

CHAPTER 33

René released his clutch, and the Delahaye leaped forward. Rudi was quicker away, the tires of his Silver Arrow searing parallel black scars onto the pavement. René shifted quickly, his tachometer needle spiking and then falling in rapid succession as he sped down the tail end of the Avenue du Bois Louis and past the first sections of the grandstands.

Into the slight right bend by the pits, Rudi was two car lengths ahead. He angled across the road to close off René from passing him. There was another brief straight, then the sharp turn at Virage de la Gare, where René clung to the right curb. As he came out of the turn, the tail of the Delahaye waggled, but he recovered and punched his accelerator, starting the climb of the long but narrow Avenue Léon Say. Such was the rush of air that his head was forced back against his seat.

Rudi streaked ahead of him, his superior power devouring the uphill straight. To their left, clinging to the side of a wedge-shaped hill dotted with palm trees, a mass of spectators witnessed the opening drama. Above them, bent over the edge of the promenade, another swell of people watched. In their light-colored summer clothes and hats, they were all but a blur of white to the drivers.

On the ascent, Rudi and René separated themselves from the

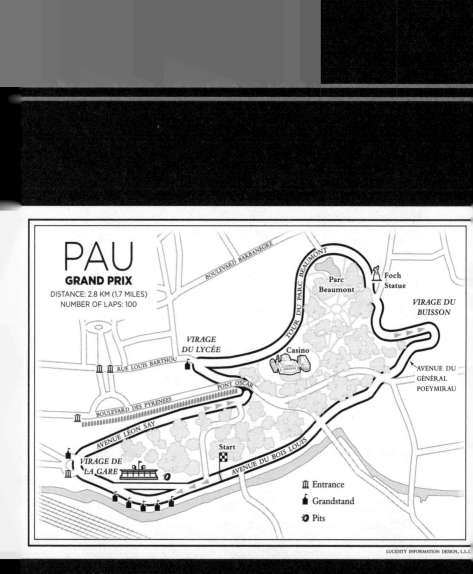

Map of the Pau race course.

others very quickly. They crossed underneath a black wrought-iron pedestrian bridge that spanned the avenue. Those lucky enough to have a place on the bridge watched the race cars flash under their feet. Rudi was first into the left-hand hairpin that passed underneath the Promenade Pont Oscar. Such was his speed as he entered into the turn that his wheels skipped across the pavement.

René followed into what was effectively a short tunnel, his eyes given only an instant to adjust to the dark before he was again in piercing daylight. Already, his initial nerves had settled. The road continued to climb, and in another brief bend he ripped through a rapid change of gears. The yawp of his engine ricocheted off the street's stone buildings.

Just as he was gathering speed, he prepared to brake in front of the imposing gray edifice of the Lycée Louis-Barthou. The Virage du Lycée was so sharp a hairpin that drivers had to take it almost at a crawl.

As Rudi came out of it, his Silver Arrow suffered what one reporter called "paralyzing wheelspin." René and Rudi were now bunched together nose to tail. A missed shift of Rudi's gears and the Delahaye would ram straight into his rear. The Mercedes swept around the Tour du Parc Beaumont, a U-shaped route around the park. This level part of the course was packed with spectators, held back by a wooden barrier.

Next, the two drivers passed the casino, an expansive cream-colored building with twin steeples. Then they roared around a looping bend lined with stacks of straw bales. The second half of the park leg featured a right–left–right chicane that left the cars' tails zigzagging across the pavement. The section was watched over by an imposing statue of Marshal Ferdinand Foch, the Allied commander whose September 1918 offensive brought World War I to an end. The French general did not blink at the sight of a German driver in the lead.

Soon enough, Rudi was hurtling downhill. René tried to keep close, thinking not only about the sloping turn he was traversing but also about the next moves he would have to make on the constantly changing course. In that, a racing driver is not unlike a billiards player, taking a shot while at the same time setting up the next one . . . and the next.

René followed the Avenue du Général Poeymirau along a line of houses perched on the edge of the descent until the Virage du Buisson. At certain moments, it looked like he and Rudi were driving in opposite directions as they took the hairpin bends down the steep hill. Then, before they could gain much speed, they downshifted gears and jogged through another chicane.

The road never seemed to straighten, and it was so narrow that René knew even a small error in movement would see his tires clip against the curb and his Delahaye swing into a stone wall. He escaped the chicane unscathed and entered the longest straight on the course: Avenue du Bois Louis. By the time he hit 100 mph, screaming by the tree-lined road toward the start, Rudi had distanced himself by almost 20 yards. This represented a fraction of time, but to those in the mostly French-populated grandstands, the separation was a dispiriting one.

Rudi finished the first lap in 1 minute 52 seconds, René a second behind. Comotti in his Delahaye was third, 9 seconds back. The others trailed in the distance. Ninety-nine laps to go.

Again, Rudi rounded the circuit in front. Again, René finished close behind. They were so close at times that their cars almost touched. As René had experienced in the past, the exhaust from the fuel belching out of the Silver Arrow made him feel like he was being slowly anesthetized, particularly since the circuit through the streets of Pau trapped the fumes. Still, he wanted to remain tight on Rudi in case Uhlenhaut had come up with some surprise change since practice to counteract the W154's poor handling of corners.

By the end of the fifth lap, René had his answer: There had been no change. Rudi continued to have trouble on the corners. His engine was simply too powerful for the course. Given that their average speed was only 55.8 mph, he had brought a cannon to a close-quarter knife fight.

In the seventh lap, René decided to try to overtake, to see if it could be done. Accelerating out of the Virage du Lycée, he gained ground on the Silver Arrow. He drew up on Rudi's tail, waiting for his moment. Then, as they took the wide bend that began the downhill run, he struck, threading through a gap on Rudi's inside and taking the lead. The nearby crowds cheered madly, and when the report came over the loudspeakers by the grandstands, they too joined the uproar. With open road ahead of him for the first time, René stamped on the accelerator and rounded the park. It was sweet to breathe fresh air again.

His Delahaye was braking well. The engine, tuned perfectly for the course, was running steady. He began to think he had a good chance of winning the race. He had proved that he could hang tight to the W154. He had proved that he could overtake it. Now all that was left for René to do was to drive the race of his life. Anything short of that, and Rudi, whose style was as consistent as a Swiss watch and who rarely made a mistake in either judgment or performance, would come out on top.

Over the next several laps, René held the lead. Each time he passed the grandstands, the crowd was on its feet, hats waving. The Silver Arrow was forever looming over his shoulder in the rearview mirror, tracking him like a predator around the course, nipping at his tail. No doubt the German star was trying to force a mistake or push René into overtaxing his vehicle.

They now had to manage interference from the other competitors, who they were beginning to lap regularly. The Maseratis driven by the Italians Antonio Negro and Dioscoride Lanza were struggling mightily on the course. Negro had already stopped twice in the pits, and by lap 10, the two leaders had already passed him three times. On the slender, twisting course populated with blind turns, the slower cars were dangerous: constantly moving obstacles that could seemingly materialize out of nowhere.

In the twelfth lap, Rudi crept up to René's side, and the two almost locked together as they zigzagged around the course, neck and neck, neither giving way to the other. They were like two gladiators in fixed combat before a crowded coliseum.

Coming down the straight to finish the fifteenth lap, René kept to a moderate pace even though he wanted to shift into fourth gear: Too much speed tempted fate.

Rudi pounced on the opportunity and overtook René's Delahaye, then almost immediately lapped Comotti in his. A groan of disappointment coursed through the stands, while the Mercedes pits cheered. Nothing and no one could rival their dominance in the straights. Rudi looked like he was ready to leave the French upstart in his wake for good. Once around the Virage de la Gare, he barreled up the hill, quickly widening his lead. At the end of the sixteenth lap, timekeepers punched their stopwatches and marveled at the reading: 1 minute 47 seconds. It was a new lap record for Pau.

By the faintness of the Mercedes engine, René knew that he was completely out of contact even before he saw the board the Delahaye crew posted, telling him he was six seconds behind. Perhaps, Rudi had been holding back after all. If René lost so much as a second per lap from his rival, the race would be over, even with the Mercedes's need to refuel. If he were to lose two seconds per circuit, Rudi would lap him completely.

René fought to bridge the gap, but by the twentieth round, Rudi maintained a five-second lead, averaging a pace of 1 minute 49 seconds. Comotti was third, Trintignant fourth, Comte George Raphaël Béthenod de Montbressieux (in Maserati) fifth—all three a distant lap behind. As predicted, the Pau Grand Prix had become a contest between Mercedes and the Million-Franc Delahaye, and the German car was showing better mettle.

Over the next five laps, Rudi widened his advantage, gaining the average of a second's gap that René had dreaded. He was maintaining his pace while René was struggling to keep up. Often, the Silver Arrow was completely out of sight, and René was unaware of how much of a separation there was until he ran past the pits where a signal board showed him the expanding, soul-crushing gap.

By the thirtieth lap, almost an hour into the hundred-lap race, Rudi had gained another second over the Delahaye. His lead was commanding but not yet insurmountable because of his expected refueling somewhere near the midpoint. To take advantage of that, René would have to avoid not only mechanical trouble but also a crash—an ever-present possibility. A single instant of lost focus, and disaster might strike. The course demanded a torturous routine of gear shifts, braking, jerks of acceleration, rapid switches of steering, and lurching slowdowns. It was tough on the cars and tougher on the drivers. Both drivers had a long battle ahead before either one could claim victory.

CHAPTER 34

Throughout Europe and beyond, motorsport fans huddled around radios in their homes and local bars, wondering what might come next in this two-man struggle. Among them was a car-crazy fourteen-year-old Jewish kid named John Weitz, who had been sent away from Berlin by his parents to study in the safety of London. For Weitz, René Dreyfus was nothing short of a "divine avenger" for his people.

All through René's Grand Prix career, racing aficionados had labeled him a "scientific driver," one who typically drove with intelligence, finesse, patience, and tactical acumen. He was also known as a driver who rarely forced his car to the breaking point and who always avoided outrageous risk—particularly after his narrow escape at Comminges in 1932.

Into the thirty-first lap, René surprised them all by charging after Rudi. He had no other choice. If he continued to lag behind, the race was over already. So he began pushing himself, all but calling out his every fervent move:

Blaze up the hill to Pont Oscar. Swerve into the sharp underpass.

Faster.

Brake before the sharp turn at the Lycée Louis-Barthou.

Faster.

Rudi roars up the hill at Pau, far in the lead.

Press the foot flat along the long spoon turn of Parc Beaumont.

Faster.

Zigzag through the chicane past the statue of Marshal Foch.

Faster.

Swoop into the curved downhill of Avenue du Général Poeymirau.

Faster.

Charge deep into the Virage du Buisson. Stick the hairpin.

Faster.

Dive into the serpentine descent toward Avenue du Bois Louis.

Faster.

Launch into the start-finish straight. Take the higher gear.

Faster.

In a ruthless sally that captivated spectators and journalists, René closed by almost half Rudi's eleven-second lead. Over the next nine laps, Rudi tried to shake René off. Every time they passed the pits, Neubauer was there, frantically waving the red-and-black flag that signaled his driver to increase his speed.

The distance between the two cars seesawed back and forth— Rudi stretching his lead in straights, René clawing it back in the corners. It was as if they were tethered by a spring that would not allow either of them to draw too far away from the other.

By the fortieth lap, in a virtuoso driving performance, René had chipped down the Silver Arrow lead to only three seconds. Comotti, their closest competitor, was two full rounds of the circuit behind. In last place, piloting a Maserati, was Lanza, who had been lapped an ignoble thirteen times.

As Rudi entered lap 42, Neubauer continued to signal him to go faster. Flushed red, he waved the flag with such fervency, it looked like the stick might snap. They both knew they needed at least half a minute to refuel, not including the precious seconds lost when entering and leaving the pits. The race was almost at the midpoint, and they had only a slim lead—far from what they needed.

Rudi felt there was nothing more he could do. On exiting turns, his wheels kept spinning out, especially now that the circuit was slicked with oil and rubber from the other cars. He would never be able to use the full potential of the car's power in the straights. His leg hurt from all the shifting and braking, and was getting burned by the hot exhaust pipe. Third gear kept slipping out. He should be winning this race. He was expected to win this race. The Reich expected it. Losing was not an option.

Again, Rudi tried to widen his lead. René hounded him at every turn, pushing relentlessly. There was no need for him to pass the Mercedes. Its pit stop would do the work for him. Through to the fiftieth lap, René allowed the Silver Arrow a couple more seconds of a lead simply to be free of its noxious fumes. Such was his confidence. Such was his control and rhythm on the course.

Rudi had tried to break him. René had broken him instead.

In lap 52, the Mercedes finally sped into the pits, and the Delahaye passed into the lead. A roar erupted from the grandstands. With a hiss of his brakes, Rudi stopped the car, and the crew sprang into action. After unscrewing the steering wheel, he climbed out of the cockpit. Neubauer was quickly beside him for a report on the car's performance. Instead, Rudi informed him that Lang should take over. He was done. The course was too tough on his leg. His calf was seared. Third gear was nettlesome. He couldn't continue.

Panic spread in the Mercedes pit. Lang was there but dressed in his street clothes. Neubauer failed to persuade Rudi to change his mind, and Lang dove into his racing overalls. While he scrambled into the cockpit, the Mercedes was topped out with fuel.

Lang fixed his cap and goggles, then darted onto the course. Over a minute had passed.

When René came back around toward the pits, a lap board posted his sizable lead of 1 minute 9 seconds over . . . Hermann Lang. Rudi had withdrawn. René was certain that he knew the reason why: Rudi could not bear to be beaten by a French car, let alone one piloted by René Dreyfus and all that was implied by that Jewish surname. Rudi might not have been an anti-Semite, but he knew that the Nazis would be displeased with him, their champion, for letting himself be beaten by a Jewish driver.

Only spurred further by the switch in drivers, René pressed harder than ever before. The race was barely half over, and Lang was a bold competitor, fresh of limb and concentration. René had been driving for 1.5 hours on the exhausting course, making hundreds of calculations each lap on how swiftly to brake, when to shift, how to angle into each and every turn. Sweat beaded on his forehead and soaked his overalls.

In lap 60, René posted one of his fastest circuits of the Pau course and expanded his lead to 1 minute 20 seconds. At this stage of the race, Lang would have had to gain two seconds for every lap until the finish to catch up with him. A *L'Auto* reporter predicted, "There is little chance that victory will escape him."

René kept to his heated pace. The German driver tried to respond, but he was frustrated by the other cars on the course, two of which had been lapped over a dozen times. By the sixty-fifth lap, René had widened his lead to 1 minute 27 seconds. Then, to everyone's shock, Lang steered into the pits. He complained about the gearbox, as Rudi had done earlier, but the mechanics could find no obvious problem.

René swept past, already into his next lap.

Neubauer ordered Lang to return to the race. Mercedes would not drop out. By the time the Silver Arrow was back on the course, René owned a three-minute lead. Undaunted by this long gap, Lang attacked—clearly capable of overcoming whatever shifting trouble had vexed him so. René slackened off a little on his speed. The race was his to lose.

By lap 74, Lang remained more than a lap behind but had reduced his gap. Over the next six laps, he knocked off another ten seconds. Some among the crowd wondered if he might be able to stage a comeback. Would René and his Delahaye hold? With each turn of the circuit, René drew back slightly on his pace, keeping an eye on the times when he passed the pits. He had set the stage to win, and now he needed only to perform his part to the end. He felt welded to the Delahaye, he and the car operating with single-minded intention.

Lap 85—2 minutes 22 seconds ahead.

Lap 89—2 minutes 14 seconds.

Lap 95—1 minute, 59 seconds.

Five more laps. René could almost taste the win now. Every time he came by the grandstands, the crowd pulsated with noise and energy.

Lang continued to chip away at his lead, but it was too vast to make much of a difference. Out of the Lycée hairpin, Lang clung at the Delahaye's tail, albeit a lap behind, no doubt attempting to force a mistake. René refused to oblige. He entered the fast straight toward the final stretch as the Silver Arrow passed him in a useless attack. The Delahaye engine rose to a deafening note as René came around to the finish.

Faroux stood on the line, arms raised overhead. In his right hand he held the checkered flag. When René crossed the finish, victorious, Faroux waved it jubilantly. As René pulled up in the pits, the grandstand gates and barricades around the course appeared to break, and a tide of people flooded around the Delahaye 145 and its driver.

René lowered his goggles onto his neck. A garland of flowers was placed on the Delahaye, and his crew handed René a fizzing bottle of champagne. Rising to the top of his seat, he drank to his victory—and theirs.

As René realized what he had done, a smile finally overtook the grim look of determination that had been fixed on his face over the past 3 hours 8 minutes 59 seconds. He had claimed a new record time for the Pau Grand Prix, and better, he had triumphed over Mercedes by an indisputable margin of almost two minutes.

The band struck up the Marseillaise, France's national anthem and rallying cry, and the crowd sang the verses with uncommon emotion:

Arise, children of the homeland,
The day of glory has arrived!
Against us, tyranny's
Bloody standard is raised!

That night, torchlight parades wound through the streets of Berlin and Vienna. The votes from the plebiscite had been counted: *Ja* won over *Nein* by a margin of more than ninety-nine to one. The Greater German Reich was now a reality, and Hitler declared on the radio that the results "surpassed all my expectations . . . For me this hour is the proudest of my life." Outside the Austrian capital, huge swastika-shaped fires burned like warning signs to the world.

René celebrated his win in Pau's Palais Beaumont, where a dinner was held in his honor, replete with champagne, speeches, and dancing under the twinkling chandeliers of the grand hall. When people congratulated him, he was humble, commenting that the stars of the "right day, the right driver, and the right car" had aligned in constellation.

The French press was far less reserved. In a string of articles, Charles Faroux could barely contain himself. "One cannot congratulate Delahaye enough for having beaten a rival as redoubtable as Mercedes-Benz . . . Could this be the dawn of a resurrection?" A *Paris Soir* editorial answered the question for him: "The success achieved in Pau by René Dreyfus and Delahaye thus marks the revival of the French sports industry." Newspaper headlines celebrated the same. "A Beautiful French Victory!" *Le Figaro* announced. "An Undisputed and Indisputable Victory!" exclaimed *L'Auto.*

British and American reporters also lauded the win. "There was something of a sensation at the Pau Grand Prix when the first race was held under the new Formula," wrote *Motor.*

"Delahaye may with good reason be proud that their twelve-cylinder car, in the hands of a driver of first-rate caliber such as Dreyfus, beat the Mercedes fair and square."

The report in *Motor Sport* read, "The first race run under the new formula was won by an unblown 4.5 liter car, in defiance of the forecasts of most people, and to the indescribable delight of thousands of Frenchmen, who stampeded across the road to congratulate their compatriot; cool, calm and unruffled René Dreyfus."

At the Hotel de France, the Daimler-Benz press team worked overtime to spin their interpretation of the ignoble loss. They tamped down the importance of the Pau Grand Prix, calling it a "dress rehearsal" while highlighting how the W154 had achieved the fastest lap and lost only because of its need to refuel. German newspapers parroted their press releases: The W154 was "flawless," Pau was merely a "regional race," and in the important events ahead, Mercedes was sure to come out on top. Privately, Alfred Neubauer and Rudi discounted the loss, but Mercedes driver Richard Seaman called it what it was: "an embarrassing defeat."

For René, Pau was his crowning achievement and, as Lucy intended, a blow against the invincibility of the German Silver Arrows. The symbolic importance of the victory was not lost on either of them, nor on the rest of the world. As the Third Reich pushed toward war, harbingers of hope were in short supply and in high demand.

AUTHOR'S NOTE

A terrific adventure awaits, but I must hurry.

Midmorning, heading north on the I-405 from Los Angeles International Airport, I am stuck in a traffic jam. A sea of vehicles of every make surrounds me: long-haul semis, boxy sedans, Denalis with tinted windows, Priuses with Uber stickers, black town cars, landscaping trucks, and the occasional zesty convertible. My own rented black GMC Terrain is one of those nondescript compact SUVs that automakers stamp out with all the cookie-cutter variation of a Ford Model T.

None of us is getting anywhere fast. Ten minutes pass at a standstill. Then twenty. According to Google Maps, I have another fifty-eight miles—or one hour and fifty-two minutes—to go until I reach Oxnard. The line of my route on the screen map looks an ugly red. Surely, they will wait for me before they ship "The Car That Beat Hitler" off to London to sit behind a velvet rope in the Victoria and Albert Museum. I try not to pound the steering wheel in frustration.

The bottleneck ahead finally loosens. Then I am cruising north on the Pacific Coast Highway. My GMC is comfortable, but

Modern-day restored Delahaye.

unexciting—a rental car obligation. Whatever churns underneath the hood, it is quiet, reasonable, and unflappable, all worthy qualities in a vehicle meant to get one safely from point A to point B.

A very different car, a restored Delahaye 145, is being readied for me in Oxnard. It is a reward—and capstone—after two years of investigation into its long-forgotten history. I wanted—and needed—to experience a sliver of what the heroes of this Grand Prix era had experienced in the cars they raced, most of all the Delahaye. In response to repeated requests, Richard Adatto, a board member and curator of sorts for the Mullin Automotive Museum, invited me for a drive in one of the four 145s ever built. The museum, in Oxnard, California, was founded by American multimillionaire and collector Peter Mullin.

I finally reach the museum parking lot. I turn into it and come

to a quick stop. Just in time. Someone calls my name as I climb out of my GMC. It is Richard, waving me over. Richard has a measured, no-nonsense demeanor that only occasionally is broken by an impish smile. In his sixties and a builder by profession, he is also an expert on prewar French cars. He leads me over to a boxy white warehouse opposite the museum.

The tapered tail of a car sticks halfway out of the warehouse door. The Delahaye 145. The many black-and-white photographs I have seen of the race car do it little justice. Painted a sky blue, the two-seater stands long, lean, and low, appearing altogether like a tiger crouched in anticipation of a leap. It is over eight decades old, yet somehow looks fresh from its racing days.

Much had passed in the intervening years.

On September 1, 1939, the Nazis invaded Poland. Soon after, France declared war on Germany, and a maelstrom swept across the globe. Less than a month later, Lucy and Laury were being driven back to Paris from their Monaco villa, when their chauffeur collided with a van. Both the Schells were seriously injured, and Laury died a month later. A heartbroken Lucy remained in the hospital and missed the funeral of her beloved husband and co-driver. At the gravesite, René Dreyfus supported the Schells' two sons.

A few months later, Lucy informed René that she planned to send him to America to compete in the Indianapolis 500. She wanted him out of the country in case the Nazis took France. While he crossed the Atlantic, Germany stormed across the border into France. There was nothing René could do but read the newspapers and shudder at the horrifying reports. René wanted to go back, but in telegram after telegram, Lucy and his brother, Maurice, urged him to stay in the United States. Paris fell soon after. Unable to speak English, his bank accounts frozen, René tried to forge a life for himself. He found a meager basement apartment in New York, and while living there, he learned his wife was having an affair with an official in the Fascist Vichy government. When Chou-Chou petitioned for divorce, her legal grounds were that René was Jewish. Then all word from France ceased. He did not know if his family was alive or dead.

After the attack at Pearl Harbor, René enlisted in the US Army. He underwent basic training at Fort Dix, New Jersey, and learned English at last. He also became an American citizen. Finally, in the spring of 1943, Staff Sergeant Dreyfus left for Europe and the war. His transport ship's newspaper made a big deal about how they had a celebrity on board: "Dreyfus was to the French people what Babe Ruth was to the Americans." He participated in the September 1943 Allied invasion of mainland Italy. He considered his service the greatest accomplishment of his life.

As soon as the South of France was liberated, in August 1944, he caught a military plane to Nice and went to his sister Suzanne's last known address. As he approached the door, he could already sense her presence. They soon were weeping in an embrace, so overcome with emotion that words failed them. Suzanne's husband ran off to find Maurice. At the news that his younger brother was not only alive but in the city that very moment, Maurice ran out of his apartment without his pants on.

When the three siblings reunited, stories of their years apart spilled out like spools of thread. Maurice and Suzanne had both participated in the French Resistance. Betrayed, Maurice had spent months in hiding, evading the Gestapo.

In the early hours of the morning, the three spoke of the future. America, René pitched, was the place for them. All three eventually settled in New York City. They started a French restaurant called Le Chanteclair that became renowned in the city.

In 1993, René was diagnosed with a heart condition. Almost ninety years old, he had an even chance of surviving open-heart surgery. The night before the operation, he spoke by telephone to a good friend in France. They relished memories of his driving years, most pointedly his 1938 win over the German Silver Arrows. At the end of their conversation, René wept and then said hopefully, "I've lived so many things . . . I've brushed with death many times. Maybe I'll make it out once again."

It was not to be. Shortly before the surgery was finished, René passed away. In accordance with his final wishes, friends spread some of his ashes at the places of his finest triumphs, including Montlhéry and Pau.

After World War II, Charles Weiffenbach attempted another revival of Delahaye, this time without Jean François, who had died of a lung disease in 1944. Now in his mid-seventies, Weiffenbach remained untiring, but the company struggled to make a profit in a crippled Europe and a French state increasingly bent toward socialism. By the mid-1950s, Monsieur Charles and Delahaye's owners were forced to merge with the French firm Hotchkiss. When this combined company was sold, mere months later, the Delahaye name disappeared into obscurity.

Sometime after the Nazi occupation of France, Lucy Schell left for the United States. She remained there until the armistice, and then she and her sons returned to Monaco. She never competed in motorsport again. The American speed queen, one of the preeminent Monte Carlo Rallyers for a decade and the first—and only—woman to own and lead a major Grand Prix racing team, faded from memory. In 1952, she died and was buried beside her beloved Laury in the cemetery in Brunoy.

After sitting out the war in Switzerland, Rudi Caracciola began racing again. When another serious accident left him all but crippled, he finally hung up his driving shoes. Mercedes then gave him a job pitching their cars to American troops stationed in Europe. Although successful in this new venture, he was drinking heavily, and he died from cirrhosis of the liver in 1959. The firm gave him a hero's funeral that whitewashed his role as a standard-bearer of the Third Reich—just as his own autobiography, published after the war, had done. No doubt, Rudi was one of the twentieth century's finest Grand Prix drivers, but most people chose to forget the devil's bargain he made to achieve this dream.

The initial fates of the four Écurie Bleue 145s owned by Lucy Schell remain murky, but she probably sold them off with the aid of Charles Weiffenbach, who took possession of them before the Nazi invasion. Two were known to have been kept together. Coachbuilder Henri Chapron disassembled them and scattered their parts deliberately about his shop amid a variety of car parts. The other two were hidden more remotely, in either barns or caves far from the capital, to keep them out of the hands of the Nazis.

After VE Day, the movements of the 145s became better documented. Like practiced detectives, a pair of Delahaye historians tracked down and assembled reams of information on the fate of each 145. The seized records from the Automobile Club de France, however, were never found.

One of the Delahayes received a postwar convertible roadster body from French coachbuilder Franay and was included in a "most beautiful cars in the world" exhibition. Eventually, a new owner, Philippe Charbonneaux, placed a sports-car body on the 145. At the fiftieth anniversary of the Million Franc Prize, in 1987, René Dreyfus had the joy of taking this restored Delahaye back onto the Montlhéry track and driving it at nerve-rattling speeds. This car was bought by another American, industrial designer Sam Mann, who placed it in his collection of "rolling sculpture" in Englewood, New Jersey.

Another of the Delahaye 145s participated in some postwar races. Then, for a long while, it sat, a half-bodied derelict, under the Montlhéry track before being moved to a French chateau an hour west of Paris. Peter Mullin and a partner purchased this Delahaye in 1987. After an expensive restoration in England, Mullin included it in his collection. He has since added the remaining two Chapron-bodied 145s to his collection as well.

A debate has long simmered among the American collectors over who owns the Delahaye 145 in which René claimed the Million Franc Prize and won the Pau Grand Prix. As with religious relics, authenticity (or proof thereof) is often beside the point to most people. It's the emotion invoked by the object that is paramount. One cannot walk around the sleek bodies of the Mullin 145s or the Mann 145—or listen to the growls of their V12s—and fail to be moved. All bring to mind a great struggle in which David conquered Goliath, and, for a moment, there were heroes again in the world.

Beside some lemon groves outside Oxnard, I fold myself into the passenger seat of the Delahaye 145. Richard shoehorns into

The Delahaye 145 found at Château du Gérier, owned by collector Serge Pozzoli.

the driver's seat next to me. A trailer had taken us and the car fifteen minutes outside Oxnard; the empty roads that threaded through the groves were a perfect place to let the race car run free.

Despite my many entreaties to drive the Delahaye myself, I was denied—and not without reason. The 145 was worth many millions of dollars, and Peter Mullin did not need an uninsured amateur seizing up its engine or pitching it into a tree. Anyway, given how tightly Richard and I are pressed together in the narrow two-seater, there is little distinction between driver and passenger.

I hitch a belt around my waist, a likely useless safety feature that René Dreyfus did not benefit from during his days piloting the Delahaye. Then, as today, one drove with neither a roll bar nor a crash helmet.

The engine fires up, smoke billows from the twin exhausts, and the thunder of the engine nearly deafens me.

Richard steps on the clutch and shifts into first gear. We roll off the gravel onto the road and make a 180-degree turn to point in the direction of a long straight. At five feet, seven inches, I am the same height that René was. My eyes barely rise over the long hood. There is no windshield. I am seated low and at a slight angle, my legs stretched out in the footwell.

Without a hint of warning, Richard vaults down the road, engine wailing as he shifts from first to second, then third. We move faster and faster, the wind sweeping back my hair. I turn to Richard. He holds the big steering wheel at ten and two, making slight, but constant, adjustments. There is that impish smile. He is loving this.

I am scared. My grip tightens on the handle. The Delahaye does not feel stable. It fights to hold a straight line. A deep ditch borders the road. A plunge there would surely be the end of things.

Richard neither brakes nor eases on the throttle. My feet press pedals that do not exist. Richard swings the wheel counterclockwise, and the tires clip the gravel edge of the road as we enter the left turn. The Delahaye hugs tight to the ground as we make the turn. Coming out of it, Richard presses on the gas, then shifts gears again. The tachometer needle swings sharply. We are now devouring an uphill climb. The engine pitches to a high scream. Quickly, we enter another turn, this one to the right. Again, the Delahaye clings to the road. We enter a long undulating straight.

A quick upshift. The Delahaye jolts ahead, faster than before, past the rows of lemon trees. Any fear fades away. The wind presses my hair back. It ripples my cheeks. The acceleration forces my upper body against the seat. The engine rises to an earsplitting howl and throbs all around me, alive. We rocket forward. I feel every dip and hump in the road but am not jarred; it is like I am welded with the Delahaye. It is the same with every shift of the gears, every tap on the brakes. Time evaporates. The world distills into the band of pavement ahead and the surrounding rush of wind and noise.

"Remarkable," I whisper. "Remarkable."

We summit a small hill, and it almost feels like we are flying.

Enzo Ferrari called racing "this life of fearful joys." I never quite understood his words until that afternoon.

SOURCES AND BIBLIOGRAPHY

ARCHIVAL AND PERSONAL PAPERS

Archives de Brunoy, France

Archives de Châtel-Guyon, France

Automobile Club Basco-Béarnais, France (ACBB)

Automobile Club de France (ACF)

Automobile Club de Nice, France (ACN)

Bundesarchiv, Germany

Cord-Duesenberg Library, United States

Daimler-Benz Archive, Germany (DBA)

Mullin Museum Archives, United States (MMA)

Simeone Foundation Museum Archive, United States

Revs Institute, United States (REVS)

Personal Papers of Richard Adatto (PPRA)

Personal Papers of Anthony Blight

Personal Papers of the Dreyfus Family (PPDF)

Personal Papers of Beverly Kimes, Cord-Duesenberg Library (PPBK)

Personal Papers of Maurice Louche (PPML)

Personal Papers of Karl Ludvigsen

Personal Papers of Maurice Phillipe

BOOKS

Abeillon, Pierre. *Talbot-Lago de course.* Paris: Vandoeuvres, 1992.

Adatto, Richard, and Diana Meredith. *Delahaye Styling and Design.* Philadelphia: Coachbuilt Press, 2006.

Adatto, Richard. *French Curves.* Oxnard, CA: Mullin Automotive Museum, 2011.

——. *From Passion to Perfection: The Story of French Streamlined Styling, 1930–39.* Paris: Éditions SPE Barthelemey, 2003.

Beadle, Tony. *Delahaye: Road Test Portfolio.* Surrey, UK: Brooklands Books, 2010.

Belle, Serge. *Blue Blood: A History of Grand Prix Racing Cars in France.* London: Frederick Warne, 1979.

Bellon, Bernard. *Mercedes in Peace and War: German Automobile Workers, 1903–1945.* New York: Columbia University Press, 1990.

Birabongse, Prince of Thailand. *Bits and Pieces.* London: Furnell and Sons, 1942.

Birkin, Sir Henry ("Tim"). *Full Throttle.* London: G. T. Foulis & Co., 1945.

Blight, Anthony. *The French Sports Car Revolution: Bugatti, Delage, Delahaye and Talbot in Competition 1934–1939.* Somerset, UK: G. T. Foulis & Co., 1990.

Blumenson, Martin. *The Vilde Affair: Beginnings of the French Resistance.* Boston: Houghton Mifflin, 1977.

Boddy, William. *Montlhéry: The Story of the Paris Autodrome.* Dorchester, UK: Veloce Publishing, 2006.

Bouzanquet, Jean Francois. *Fast Ladies: Female Racing Drivers from 1888 to 1970.* London: Veloce Publishing, 2009.

Bradley, W. F. *Ettore Bugatti.* Abingdon, UK: Motor Racing Publications, 1948.

Brauchitsch, Manfred von. *Ohne Kampf Kein Siege.* Berlin: Verlag der Nation, 1966.

Bretz, Hans. *Bernd Rosemeyer: Ein Leben Für den Deutschen Sport.* Berlin: Wilhelm Limpert-Verlag, 1938.

Bretz, Hans. *Mannschaft und Meisterschaft: Eine Bilanz der Grand-Prix-Formel 1934–1937.* Stuttgart: Daimler-Benz AG, 1938.

Bugatti, L'Ebe. *The Bugatti Story.* Philadelphia: Chilton Book Co., 1967.

Bullock, Alan. *Hitler: A Study in Tyranny.* New York: Bantam Books, 1958.

Bullock, John. *Fast Women: The Drivers Who Changed the Face of Motor Racing.* London: Robson Books, 2002.

Burden, Hamilton T. *The Nuremberg Rallies: 1923–39.* London: Pall Mall Press, 1967.

Cancellieri, Gianna. *Auto Union—Die Großen Rennen 1934–39.* Hanover: Schroeder and Weise, 1939.

Canestrini, Giovanni. *Uomini e Motori.* Monza: Nuova Massimo, 1957.

Caracciola, Rudolf. *A Racing Car Driver's World.* New York: Farrar, Straus and Giroux, 1961.

——. *Rennen—Sieg—Rekorde!* Stuttgart: Union Deutsche Verlagsgesellschaft, 1943.

Carter, Bruce. *Nuvolari and Alfa Romeo.* New York: Coward McCann, 1968.

Cernuschi, Giovanni. *Corse per il mondo.* Milan: Editoriale Sportiva, 1947.

Cernuschi, Count Giovanni. *Nuvolari.* New York: William Morrow, 1960.

Chakrabongse, Prince Chula. *Dick Seaman: A Racing Champion.* Los Angeles: Floyd Clymer, 1948.

———. *Road Star Hat Trick: Being an Account of Two Seasons of "B. Bira" the Racing Motorist in 1937 and 1938.* London: G. T. Foulis & Co., 1944.

Cholmondeley-Tapper, Thomas Pitt. *Amateur Racing Driver.* London: G. T. Foulis & Co., 1966.

Cohin, Edmond. *Historique de la course automobile.* Paris: Éditions Lariviere, 1966.

Court, William. *A History of Grand Prix Motor Racing, 1906–1951.* London: Macdonald, 1966.

Daley, Robert. *Cars at Speed: Classic Stories from Grand Prix's Golden Age.* New York: Collier Books, 1961.

Darmendrail, Pierre. *Le Grand Prix de Pau: 1899–1960.* Paris: La Librairie du Collectionneur, 1992.

Day, Uwe. *Silberpfeil und Hakenkreuz: Autorennsport im Nationalsozialismus.* Berlin: Bebra Verlag, 2005.

Dick, Robert. *Auto Racing Comes of Age: A Transatlantic View of Cars, Drivers and Speedways, 1900–1925.* London: McFarland & Co., 2013.

Domarus, Max, *Hitler: Speeches and Proclamations.* Mundelein, IL: Bolchazy-Carducci Publishers, 1990.

Dorizon, Jacques, Francois Peigney, and Jean-Pierre Dauliac. *Delahaye: Le Grand Livre.* Paris: EPA Éditions, 1995.

Doyle, Gary. *Carlo Demand in Motion and Color 1895–1956.* Boston: Racemaker Press, 2007.

Dreyfus, René, with Beverly Rae Kimes. *My Two Lives: Race Driver to Restaurateur.* Tucson: Aztec Corp., 1983.

Dugdale, John. *Great Motor Sport of the Thirties: A Personal Account by John Dugdale.* London: Wilton House Gentry, 1977.

Earl, Cameron. *Quicksilver: An Investigation into the Development of German Grand Racing Cars 1934–1939.* London: HMSO, 1996.

Ferrari, Enzo. *My Terrible Joys.* London: Hamish Hamilton, 1963.

Francois-Poncet, André. *The Fateful Years: Memoirs of a French Ambassador in Berlin, 1931–38.* New York: Howard Fertig, 1972.

Frilling, Christoph. *Elly Beinhorn und Bernd Rosemeyer: Kleiner Grenzverkehr zwischen Resistenz und Kumpanei im Nationalsozialismus.* Frankfurt: Peter Lang, 2009.

Gautier, Jean, and Jean-Pierre Altounian. *Brunoy: Memoire en Images.* France: Éditions Alan Sutton, 1996.

Goebbels, Joseph. *Die Tagebücher.* Munich: K. G. Saur Verlag, 2000.

Gregor, Neil. *Daimler-Benz in the Third Reich.* New Haven, CT: Yale University Press, 1998.

Hamilton, Charles. *Leaders and Personalities of the Third Reich.* San Jose, CA: R. James Bender Publishing, 1998.

Helck, Peter. *Great Auto Races.* New York: Harry Abrams, 1975.

Herzog, Bodo. *Unter dem Mercedes-Stern: Die Große Zeit der Silberpfeile.* Preetz, Germany: Ernst Gerdes Verlag, 1966.

Hildenbrand, Laura. *Seabiscuit: Three Men and a Racehorse.* New York: Random House, 2001.

Hilton, Christopher. *Grand Prix Century: The First 100 Years of the World's Most Glamorous and Dangerous Sport.* Somerset, UK: Haynes Publishing, 2005.

———. *Hitler's Grands Prix in England: Donington 1937 and 1938.* Somerset, UK: Haynes Publishing, 1999

———. *How Hitler Hijacked World Sport: The World Cup, the Olympics, the Heavyweight Championship, and the Grand Prix.* Stroud, UK: History Press, 2012.

———. *Inside the Mind of the Grand Prix Driver.* Somerset, UK: Haynes Publishing, 2001.

———. *Nuvolari.* Derby, UK: Breedon Books Publishing, 2003.

Hochstetter, Dorothee. *Motorisierung und "Volksgemeinschaft": Das Nationalsozialistische Kraftfahrkorps (NSKK) 1931–1945.* Munich: R. Oldenbourg Verlag, 2005.

Hodges, David. *The Monaco Grand Prix.* London: Temple Press Books, 1964.

Howe, Lord Earl. *Motor Racing.* London: Seeley Service & Co., 1939.

Jellinek-Mercedes, Guy. *My Father, Mr. Mercedes.* London: Chilton Book Co., 1961.

Jenkinson, Denis. *The Grand Prix Mercedes-Benz, Type W125, 1937.* New York: Arco Publishing, 1970.

———. *The Racing Driver: The Theory and Practice of Fast Driving.* London: BT Batsford, 1958.

Jolly, Francois. *Delahaye: Course, sport & tourisme V12.* Nimes, France: Éditions du Palmier, 1980.

——. *Delahaye: Sport et prestige.* Paris: Jacques Grancher, 1981.

Kershaw, Ian. *Hitler: 1936–1945 Nemesis.* New York: W. W. Norton, 2000.

Keys, Barbara J. *Globalizing Sport: National Rivalry and International Community in the 1930s.* Cambridge, MA: Harvard University Press, 2006.

Kimes, Beverly. *The Star and the Laurel: The Centennial History of Daimler, Mercedes, and Benz.* Montvale, NJ: Mercedes-Benz of North America, 1986.

King, Bob. *The Brescia Bugatti.* Mulgrave, Australia: Images Publishing Group, 2006.

Klemperer, Victor. *I Will Bear Witness 1933–1941: A Diary of the Nazi Years.* New York: Modern Library, 1999.

——. *The Language of the Third Reich: A Philologist's Notebook.* London: Athlone Press, 2000.

Labric, Roger. *Robert Benoist: Champion du Monde.* Paris: Edicta Paris, 2008.

Lang, Hermann. *Grand Prix Driver.* London: G. T. Foulis & Co., 1953.

Larsen, Peter, with Ben Erickson. *Talbot-Lago Grand Sport: The Car from Paris.* Copenhagen: Dalton, Watson Fine Books, 2012.

Laux, James. *In First Gear: The French Automobile Industry to 1914.* Montreal: McGill-Queen's University Press, 1976.

Lemerie, Jean-Louis, and Emmanuel Piat. *Histoire de l'Automobile Club de France.* Paris: Alcyon Media Groupe, 2012.

Liddell Hart, B. H. *History of the Second World War.* Old Saybrook, CT: Konecky & Konecky, 1970.

Lottman, Herbert. *The Fall of Paris: June 1940.* London: Sinclair-Stevenson, 1992.

Louche, Maurice. *1895–1995: Un Siècle de Grands Pilotes Français.* Nimes, France: Éditions du Palmier, 1995.

——. *Le Rallye Monte-Carlo au XXᵉ Siècle.* 2 vols. Monaco: L'Automobile-Club de Monaco, 2001.

Ludvigsen, Karl. *Classic Grand Prix Cars: The Front-Engined Formula 1 Era 1906–1960.* Gloucestershire, UK: Sutton Publishing, 2000.

——. *Mercedes-Benz Racing Cars.* Newport Beach, CA: Bond/Parkhurst Books, 1974.

——. *The V12 Engine: The Untold Story of the Technology, Evolution, Performance, and Impact of All V12-Engined Cars.* Somerset, UK: Haynes Publishing, 2005.

Lyndon, Barre. *Grand Prix.* London: John Miles, 1935.

Malino, Frances, and Bernard Wasserstein. *The Jews in Modern France.* Lebanon, NH: University Press of New England, 1985.

Marc-Antoine, Colin. *Delahaye 135*. Paris: ETAI, 2003.

Mays, Raymond. *Split Seconds: My Racing Years*. London: G. T. Foulis & Co., 1951.

Mitchell, Allan. *Nazi Paris: History of an Occupation, 1940–1944*. New York: Berghahn Books, 2010.

Moity, Christian. *Grand Prix Automobile de Monaco*. Vol. 1, *1929–1955*. Besançon, France: Éditions d'Art/J. P. Barthelemy, 1996.

Molter, Günther. *German Racing Cars and Drivers: Pre-War and Post-War*. Los Angeles: Floyd Clymer, 1950.

———. *Rudolf "Caratsch" Caracciola: Außergewöhnlicher Rennfahrer und Eiskalter Taktiker*. Stuttgart: Motor Buch Verlag, 1997.

Mommsen, Hanx. *The Rise and Fall of Weimar Democracy*. Chapel Hill: University of North Carolina Press, 1996.

Monkhouse, George. *Grand Prix Racing: Facts and Figures*. London: G. T. Foulis & Co., 1950.

———. *Motor Racing with Mercedes-Benz*. Los Angeles: Floyd Clymer, 1945.

Moretti, Valerio. *Grand Prix Tripoli*. Milan: Automobilia, 1994.

———. *When Nuvolari Raced . . .* Dorset, UK: Veloce Publishing, 1994.

Neubauer, Alfred. *Speed Was My Life*. New York: Clarkson Potter, 1958.

Neue Deutsche Biographie. Vol. 11. Berlin: Duncker & Humblot, 1977.

Nicholas, Lynn. *The Rape of Europa: The Fate of Europe's Treasures in the Third Reich and the Second World War*. New York: Alfred A. Knopf, 1995.

Nixon, Chris. *Kings of Nürburgring*. Middlesex, UK: Transport Bookman Publications, 2005.

———. *Racing the Silver Arrows: Mercedes-Benz versus Auto Union 1934–1939*. Oxford: Osprey, 1986.

Nolan, William. *Men of Thunder: Fabled Daredevils of Motor Sport*. New York: G. P. Putnam's Sons, 1964.

Nye, Doug, and Geoffrey Goddard. *Dick and George: The Seaman-Monkhouse Letters, 1936–1939*. London: Palawan Press, 2002.

Orsini, Luigi, and Franco Zagari. *Maserati: Una Storia nell Storia*. Milan: Emmeti Grafica, 1980.

Paris, Jean-Michel, and William Mearns. *Jean-Pierre Wimille: A Bientôt la Revanche*. Paris: Drivers, 2002.

Pascal, Dominique. *Les Grandes Heures de Montlhéry*. Boulogne-Billancourt: ETAI, 2004.

Pohl, Hans, Stephanie Habeth-Allhorn, and Beate Brüninghaus. *Die Daimler-Benz AG in den Jahren 1933 bis 1945.* Stuttgart: Franz Steiner Verlag, 1986.

Pomeroy, Laurence. *The Grand Prix Car: 1906–1939.* Abingdon, UK: Motor Racing Publications, 1949.

Pritchard, Anthony. *Silver Arrows in Camera: A Photographic Portrait of the Mercedes-Benz and Auto Union Grand Prix Teams.* Somerset, UK: Haynes Publishing, 2008.

Purdy, Ken. *The Kings of the Road.* London: Anchor Press, 1957.

Rao, Rino. *Rudolf Caracciola: Una vita per le corse.* Bologna, Italy: Edizioni ASI Service, 2015.

Reuss, Eberhard. *Hitler's Motor Racing Battles: The Silver Arrows Under the Swastika.* Somerset, UK: Haynes Publishing, 2006.

Rolt, L.T.C. *Horseless Carriage: The Motor-Car in England.* London: Constable Publishers, 1950.

Rosbottom, Ronald C. *When Paris Went Dark: The City of Light under German Occupation, 1940–1944.* New York: Little, Brown and Co., 2014.

Rosemann, Ernst. *Um Kilometer und Sekunden.* Stuttgart: Union Deutsche Verlagsgesellschaft, 1938.

Rosemeyer, Elly Einhorn, and Chris Nixon. *Rosemeyer! A New Biography.* Middlesex, UK: Transport Bookman Publishers, 1986.

Ruesch, Hans. *The Racer.* New York: Ballantine Books, 1953.

Sachs, Harvey, ed. *The Letters of Arturo Toscanini.* New York: Alfred A. Knopf, 2002.

Saward, Joe. *The Grand Prix Saboteurs.* London: Morienval Press, 2006.

Scheller, Wolfgang, and Thomas Pollak. *Rudolf Uhlenhaut: Ingenieur und Gentleman.* Königswinter, Germany: HEEL Verlag, 2015.

Setright, L. J. K. *The Designers: Great Automobiles and the Men Who Made Them.* Chicago: Follett Publishing, 1976.

Seymour, Miranda. *Bugatti Queen: In Search of a French Racing Legend.* New York: Random House, 2004.

Shirer, William L. *Berlin Diary: The Journal of a Foreign Correspondent 1934–1941.* New York: Alfred A. Knopf, 1941.

———. *The Rise and Fall of the Third Reich: A History of Nazi Germany.* New York: Simon & Schuster, 1990.

Stevenson, Peter. *Driving Forces: Grand Prix Racing Season Caught in the Maelstrom of the Third Reich.* Cambridge, UK: Bentley Publishers, 2000.

Stobbs, William. *Les Grandes Routieres: France's Classic Grand Tours.* Somerset,
UK: Haynes Publishing, 1990.

Stuck, Hans. *Männer hinter Motoren: Ein Rennfahrer erzählt.* Berlin: Drei Masken
Verlag, 1935.

Stuck, Hans, and E. G. Burggaller. *Motoring Sport.* London: G. T. Foulis & Co., 1937.

Symons, H. E. *Monte Carlo Rally.* London: Methuen & Co., 1936.

Taruffi, Piero. *The Technique of Motor Racing.* Cambridge, MA: Robert Bentley, 1961.

Taylor, Blain. *Hitler's Engineers: Fritz Todt and Albert Speer—Master Builders of the
Third Reich.* Philadelphia: Casemate, 2010.

Tissot, Jean-Paul. *Figoni & Delahaye: 1934–1954: La haute couture automobile.*
Anthony, France: ETA, 2013.

Tragatsch, Erwin. *Die Großen Rennjahre 1919–1939.* Stuttgart: Hallwag Verlag, 1973.

Tucoo-Chala, Pierre. *Histoire de Pau.* Toulouse: Univers de la France, 2000.

Venables, David. *First among Champions: The Alfa Romeo Grand Prix.* Somerset,
UK: Haynes Publishing, 2000.

———. *French Racing Blue: Drivers, Cars and Triumphs of French Motor Racing.*
London: Ian Allan Publishing, 2009.

Walkerley, Rodney. *Grand Prix 1934–1939.* Abingdon, UK: Motor Racing
Publications, 1948.

Walter, Gerard. *Paris under the Occupation.* New York: Orion Press, 1960.

Weber, Eugen. *The Hollow Years: France in the 1930s.* New York: W. W. Norton, 1994.

Weitz, Eric D. *Weimar Germany: Promise and Tragedy.* Princeton: Princeton
University Press, 2007.

Wolff, Marion Freyer. *The Shrinking Circle: Memories of Nazi Berlin, 1933–1939.*
New York: UAHC Press, 1989.

Yates, Brock. *Enzo Ferrari: The Man, the Cars, the Races, the Machine.* New York:
Doubleday, 1991.

Zagari, Franco. *Tazio Nuvolari.* Milan: Automobilia, 1992.

PERIODICALS/NEWSPAPERS

ACF magazine (French)

Alfa Corse magazine (Italian)

Auto Age

Auto Moto Retro (French)

Auto Passion (French)

Auto Retro

Autocar

Automobile Quarterly

Automobilia (French)

Autosport

Bugantics

Car and Driver

Club Delahaye Bulletin (French)

Das Auto (German)

Englebert (French)

Horizons

Il Littoriale (Italian)

L'Actualité Automobile (French)

L'Auto (French)

L'Auto Italiana (Italian)

L'Automobile Sur la Côte d'Azur (French)

L'Équipe (French)

L'Intransigent (French)

La Dépêche (French)

La Fanatatique de Automobile (French)

La Vie Automobile (French)

Le Journal (French)

Light Car

La Locomotion Automobile (French)

Le Figaro (French)

Locomotive Engineer's Journal

Match (French)

Moteurs Course

Motor

Motor (German)

Motor Italia (Italian)

Motor Sport

Motor und Sport (German)

Motorspeed

Old Cars

Omnia (French)

Paris Soir (French)

Pur Sang

RACI (Italian)

Revue Automobile Club Feminin (French)

Road and Track

Speed

Sports Car Graphic

Sports Car Guide

Sports Car Illustrated

Sport Review's Motorspeed

Torque

Veteran and Vintage

SOURCE NOTES

In any history, I often draw on a dozen or more sources for every written page. Rather than an exhaustive endnotes section detailing each one, I'd rather highlight key material—and in that way offer a short instructive guide to how such narrative works are crafted from the underlying material. In addition, I provide references for all quotes used in the book and particular sections where more comprehensive sourcing—or insight—is worthwhile to know.

Primary sources are the most critical for any new history. As much as possible, I draw on eyewitness accounts, memoirs, diaries, documents, speech transcripts, audiotaped interviews, and even video. This firsthand evidence is as close to the unvarnished truth as one can trust while writing such a work. Thankfully, for *The Racers*, I had a rich trove to use.

Of particular note for René, I had a lengthy interview transcript between him and historian Jean Paul Caron, which was never published; original audio recording between René and the co-writer of his autobiography, Beverly Rae Kimes; the said autobiography, *My Two Lives*; and a long list of firsthand interviews with René in a range of newspapers and magazines.

For Rudi Caracciola and Mercedes, I relied on Rudi's memoir, *A Racing Car Driver's World*, one written by Alfred Neubauer titled *Speed Was My Life*, several memoirs by Rudi's teammates

Manfred von Brauchitsch and Hermann Lang, and a bunch of internal documents from the Daimler-Benz Archive in Stuttgart.

Lucy and Delahaye were more challenging to source, but there were a number of interview/documents reproduced in the Delahaye Club Bulletin, and the contemporaneous newspapers *L'Auto* and *L'Intransigent* (published in Paris at the time) provide first-hand interviews with Lucy Charles, Weiffenbach, and Jean Francois. Furthermore, on Delahaye, historians Richard Adatto and André Vaucourt generously shared with me a range of internal documents from the company, including blueprints of the cars, production lists, and other material.

In addition, I relied heavily on period newspapers and magazines, especially when chronicling the various races and details of the drivers on and off the course. Given that the authors of these materials were there at the time and knew the principals well, they provide excellent portraits of events, often with the kind of visceral, in-the-scene details that simply are not available elsewhere. As noted in the bibliography, I tapped a range of British, French, Italian, and German publications. Those that were especially helpful were again *L'Auto*, but also *Motor Sport*, *Autocar*, *Motor*, *Paris Soir*, *Motor Italia*, and *Motor und Sport*. *The Racers* could not have been written without the extremely deep bench of auto racing publications at the time—and the fine quality of writing from their journalists.

Last, but often not least, came secondary sources, chiefly histories written about this period. Once one dives deep into a subject, they can begin to see which authors are simply regurgitating what others have already written—and those who have done a tremendous amount of mining of primary material in their own right. I always lean on the latter rather than the former, of course. Only after reading everything—and inspecting the endnotes of each book—can one discern the difference between the two. Since all the principals of this story had died long before I started this project, I needed to benefit from the historians/authors who had interviewed or known René, Lucy, Rudi, and the Delahaye company and who had plumbed archives not readily available any longer.

In this arena, there were a number of particular standouts. First and foremost, Anthony Blight's *The French Sports Car Revolution* was an absolute treasure in providing insight into this narrative, particularly the development of the 145, the genesis of Écurie Bleue, and René and Lucy's involvement from start to finish. François Jolly's *Delahaye: Sport et Prestige* was also key. I also benefited greatly from a number of fine histories on Daimler-Benz and the influence of the Third Reich on the automotive scene at the time, namely works detailed in the bibliography by Uwe Day, Dorothee Hochstetter, Günther Molter, George Monkhouse, Rino Rao, and Eberhard Reuss.

Finally, not all such secondary material needs to be found in a book. One of the best, most accurate sources of information on the various races/drivers/cars/courses of this period has been collected online by Leif Snellman. His website—The Golden Era of Grand Prix Racing—is unparalleled, and he details the various primary and secondary material he used to chronicle auto racing in the 1930s.

I hope this was helpful for those interested in further investigating this era—or simply as a short primer on the process of researching such a book. One of the true joys of being an author of narrative history is the detective work in collecting all the evidence of events past.

PROLOGUE

"a cruel machine . . .": Walter, *Paris Under the Occupation*, p. 13.

"With bicycles and bundles . . .": Lottman, *The Fall of Paris*, p. 143.

In an automobile factory: Dorizon, Peigney, and Dauliac, *Delahaye*, p. 60; undated news clip, PPBK; Charles Fleming, "A Classic Car Mystery," *Los Angeles Times*, November 2, 2015; Mullin Automotive Museum, *Delahaye Type 145* (brochure), MMA; notes of André Vaucourt, in the author's possession; Lew Gotthainer, letter to William Smith, December 6, 1971, PPRA. The fate of the Delahaye 145s during the war is rife with contradicting stories and apocryphal legend, and the details of which of the four cars raced where is debated among Delahaye experts to this day.

"swarm of bees": Lottman, *The Fall of Paris*, p. 174.

"DEUTSCHLAND SIEGT AN ALLEN FRONTEN": Mitchell, *Nazi Paris*, p. 13.

One day early in the occupation: Richard Adatto, interview with the author, Seattle, 2017; Lemerie and Piat, *Histoire de l'Automobile Club de France*, p. 45. The story of the theft of the ACF archives derives from an interview with the keen Delahaye historian Richard Adatto. Years ago, he met with the ACF librarian profiled in this scene. The librarian recounted to Richard the tale of the theft. Confirmation of the disappearance of the archives comes from Lemerie and Piat's book, among others.

"Bring me all the race files": Adatto, interview with the author.

CHAPTER 1

"a stare of searing intensity . . .": *Sports Car Graphic*, September 1974.

Preparing to crank: Ted West, in "Rising to Greatness," *Road and Track*, March 1987, interviews Dreyfus about his 1926 hill climb career. It's a superb article with great details, not only on what Dreyfus thought and felt but also on the experiences (sounds, sights, smells) of that day. This scene, including the *blaaattt* and *rrrraapppp* of the Bugatti engine, draws on this article.

CHAPTER 2

"child with a new and better toy.": Dreyfus and Kimes, *My Two Lives*, p. 16.

"Come on, we have some work . . .": *Auto Age*, August 1956; *Sport Review's Motorspeed*, (no month) 1953, Dreyfus Magazine Scrapbook, PPDF; *Pur Sang*, Spring 1980; Moity, *Grand Prix Automobile de Monaco*, 1930, pp. 4–8.

Early the next morning: This account of the overall race is drawn from a number of sources, most with first-person interviews of Dreyfus. Of particular note, I am indebted to Leif Snellman and his website, The Golden Era of Grand Prix Racing, about racing in the 1930s. See the website's 1930 Monaco Grand Prix entry, http://www.kolumbus.fi/leif.snellman/gp3002.htm#9. Other sources include: *L'Intransigent*, April 2–10, 1930; *L'Auto*, April 2–10, 1930; *Auto Age*, August 1956; Moity, *Grand Prix Automobile de Monaco*, 1930, pp. 4–8; *Sports Car Graphic* (Monaco Public Relations), PPRA; *Road and Track*, September 1980; *Autocar*, April 11, 1930; *Motor Sport*, May 1930.

"Don't force too much . . .": *Sport Review's Motorspeed*, (no month) 1953.

"multicolored serpent": Court, *History of Grand Prix Motor Racing*, p. 189.

"dive into a dull, stone-side ravine": Lyndon, *Grand Prix*, p. 10.

"Be very careful . . .": *Road and Track*, September 1930.

CHAPTER 3

The concept of a self-propelled: This history of the automobile and the development of motor racing is based on a range of reading, but most notably: Laux, *In First Gear*; Daley, *Cars at Speed*; Rolt, *Horseless Carriage*; Ludvigsen, *Mercedes-Benz Racing Cars*.

"boiled from the waist down . . .": Birkin, *Full Throttle*, p. 10.

CHAPTER 4

Rudi found: Alice Caracciola, "Memories of a Racing Driver's Wife," *Automobile Quarterly*, Summer 1968. This short memoir by Rudi's wife provides one of the finest views into the interior life of the famed driver.

"You're not very talkative": Molter, *Rudolf "Caratsch" Caracciola*, pp. 30–40.

"Quick, man!": *Road and Track*, January 1961.

Rudi tore down: Quotes and scene from his 1926 AVUS race from *Das Auto*, July 15, 1926; "Mercedes beim Grossen Preis von Deutschland," 652, DBA; Caracciola, *Racing Car Driver's World*, pp. 35–41; Neubauer, *Speed Was My Life*, pp. 5–6; photographs, Grossen Preis von Deutschland, AVUS 1926, 93/652. DBA.

CHAPTER 5

"It's finished": Neubauer, *Speed Was My Life*, p. 16.

Shortly after Rudi's return: Caracciola, *Racing Car Driver's World*, pp. 160–63; Neubauer, *Speed Was My Life*, pp. 29–30; Stuck and Burggaller, *Motoring Sport*, pp. 162–63; Rao, *Rudolf Caracciola*, pp. 104–10. Like many of the firsthand accounts that relate to Hitler, the stories change, the impressions alter, depending on whether they were written before or after the war. Of note here, the Stuck and Burggaller book, published prewar, relates an article from Caracciola that states how impressed, and what an honor it was, to be in the presence of Hitler. His later memoir has a very different tenor.

"I've got to drive . . .": Caracciola, *Racing Car Driver's World*, p. 56.

"As light-footed . . .": Ibid., p. 57.

CHAPTER 6

"So what if their car . . .": *Le Journal*, January 15–21, 1932. This is an incredible series of vivid accounts by Jacques Marsillac of his journey with Lucy and Laury Schell during the Monte Carlo Rally. All quoted dialogue derives from this account.

"While she grew up . . .": Blight, *French Sports Car Revolution*, p. 86.

"I am American": *Paris Soir*, May 1, 1938.

"His life seems . . .": Blight, *French Sports Car Revolution*, p. 86.

CHAPTER 7

In the early hours of Saturday: *Le Journal*, January 15–21, 1932. As before, all dialogue was sourced from the Marsillac series. In addition, the author benefited from accounts in *Motor Sport*, February 1932; *Autocar*, January 12, 1932; *Motor*, January 1932; and *L'Auto*, January 10–23, 1932.

"Their names?": Blight, *French Sports Car Revolution*, pp. 84–85.

At an extraordinary meeting: This board meeting—and the revolution at
  Delahaye—is well documented in the following sources, including
  dialogue—*Automobile Quarterly*, Summer 1967; Bradley, *Ettore
  Bugatti*, p. 60; Marc-Antoine, *Delahaye 135*, pp. 11–13; Adatto,
  Delahaye Styling, p. 213; Dorizon, Peigney, and Dauliac, *Delahaye*, p. 33;
  Jolly, *Delahaye*.

CHAPTER 8

"It's over,": Draft of a preface by René Dreyfus for Luigi Orsini Franco Zagari's
  book *Maserati: Una storia nell storia*. November 1978, PPBK. This is a
  remarkable, extended version of the final preface that Dreyfus delivered for
  Orsini and Zagari, *Maserati*.

Later that summer: *La Dépêche*, August 15, 1932; *Motor Sport*, September
  1932; *L'Auto*, August 15, 1932; *L'Automobile sur la Côte d'Azur*, January
  1934. The chronicle of his crash was well documented in the contemporaneous
  press.

"hovered around us.": Michel Ribet, interview with the author, Comminges, France,
  2018.

René loved his life: *Sports Car Graphic*, September 1984; *Road and Track*,
  September 1980; *L'Automobile sur la Côte d'Azur*, January 1934; Ribet, interview
  with the author. Often it is challenging to get at the heart of what these
  individuals felt and thought over the course of their careers. René was unusually
  up front about it in a series of interviews.

"I'm ready": Original interviews between Dreyfus and Kimes, PPBK.

CHAPTER 9

"personal confidant": Pohl, Habeth-Allhorn, and Brüninghaus, *Die Daimler-Benz
  AG in den Jahren*, pp. 36–38.

"he will be able . . .": Bellon, *Mercedes in Peace and War*, p. 219.

"profound speech": Reuss, *Hitler's Motor Racing Battles*, p. 67.

"Highly esteemed Herr Reich Chancellor": Ibid., p. 69; minutes of
  March 10, 1933, Daimler-Benz board meeting, Kissel Files, DBA.

"You know . . .": Caracciola, *Racing Car Driver's World*, p. 60.

The two drivers shot: *L'Intransigent*, April 22, 1933; *Motor Sport*, June 1933; *Autocar*, April 28, 1933; *L'Auto*, April 21, 1933; Caracciola, *Racing Car Driver's World*, pp. 60–64. Rudi's memoir is particularly evocative in describing this crash and the blur of emotions and physical agony that he experienced. It is a very fine piece of writing.

CHAPTER 10

It was awful: Unsourced and undated interview with René Dreyfus, René Dreyfus Scrapbooks, MMA. Ferrari, *My Terrible Joys*, p. 89; Brauchitsch, *Ohne Kampf Kein Siege*, p. 46. The mental state of the drivers—and their reactions to the danger and death—is a profoundly interesting subject. In fact, they referred to ambulances at the time as "bone collectors" (Caracciola, *Rennen*, p. 53) because accidents were so lethal.

"Of course, I can": Caracciola, *Racing Car Driver's World*, pp. 71–75; Caracciola, *Rennen*, pp. 75–76; Neubauer, *Speed Was My Life*, pp. 52–53. As was typical, Neubauer tended to conflate scenes. Taken with Caracciola's two memoirs, the author has done his best to separate the conversations and meeting that occurred between November 1933 and January 1934.

"Fit and well again?": Ibid.

The theory behind: "Der Mercedes-Benz Rennwagen, ein Meisterwerk deutscher Technik," internal Mercedes-Benz report, DBA; Ludvigsen research notes, personal papers of Karl Ludvigsen, REVS; *Road and Track*, December 1971. For those seeking further information on the development of the W25, this *Road and Track* article by Karl Ludvigsen, the preeminent Mercedes-Benz historian, is a minutely detailed investigation of its design and characteristics.

CHAPTER 11

"best Delahaye rally driver . . .": Blight, *French Sports Car Revolution*, p. 91.

In motorsport, Lucy: To understand better the world and challenges of the speed queens of this early era, there are no two better books than Bullock, *Fast Women*, and Bouzanquet, *Fast Ladies*.

"weak and delicate . . .": *La Vie Automobile*, September 25, 1929.

"only attentive to the aesthetic factor": news clip of undated editorial, René Dreyfus Scrapbooks, MMA.

"They chase after us . . .": Ribet, interview with the author.

"admirable virtuosity": *L'Intransigent*, April 1, 1934.

CHAPTER 12

"For me, there had to be . . .": *Automobile Quarterly*, Summer 1968; Caracciola,
    Racing Car Driver's World, p. 80.

"the tearing exhaust note . . .": *Motor Sport*, April 1934.

"his country's cars to be supreme . . .": Dreyfus and Kimes, *My Two Lives*, p. 52.

"Well, that's too bad. . . .": *Automobile Quarterly*, Summer 1967.

"the noisiest car on earth": Ludvigsen, *Mercedes-Benz Racing Cars*, p. 121.

"The mighty German assault . . .": *Motor Trend*, March 1939.

CHAPTER 13

"never bending, never capitulating": Feldpost No. 42, February 7, 1942, NS 24/846,
    Bundesarchiv; Hamilton, *Leaders and Personalities of the Third Reich*, pp. 287–88;
    Hilton, *How Hitler Hijacked World Sport*, p. 12; Hochstetter, *Motorisierung und*
    "Volksgemeinschaft," p. 124.

"man of action": Reuss, *Hitler's Motor Racing Battles*, p. 101.

"battle for the motorization of Germany": Hochstetter, *Motorisierung und*
    "Volksgemeinschaft," p. 2.

"the cavalry of the future": Ibid., p. 101.

In return, the Nazi government: "Bericht uber Kosten fur den Bau und die
    Entiwckelung eines neuen Rennwagentyps," November 9, 1934, DBA; Reuss,
    Hitler's Motor Racing Battles, pp. 81–83. In his well-researched book, Reuss
    details how Mercedes and Auto Union received far more than previously
    reported. The Daimler-Benz archive records match his findings.

CHAPTER 14

"the Old Man": René Dreyfus, letter to Maurice Louche, 1990, PPML.

"No, Dreyfus was second": Dreyfus and Kimes, *My Two Lives*, p. 53.

"René, you could be one of the greatest drivers in the world . . .": *Sports Car Guide*,
    September 1959; Dreyfus and Kimes, *My Two Lives*, p. 51; *Automobile Quarterly*,
    Summer 1967. Dreyfus recounts this same conversation almost verbatim in these

three separate publications. The author has folded the thrust of Costantini's advice into this single statement.

CHAPTER 15

"Racing is and always will be . . .": Hochstetter, *Motorisierung und "Volksgemeinschaft,"* p. 308.

"enemies of the Reich": Brauchitsch, *Ohne Kampf Kein Siege*, pp. 101–4. These are some remarkably disturbing passages from Brauchitsch, but they provide an excellent window into the mind-set of the drivers in how they thought about the crimes of the state.

"fourth shore": Moretti, *Grand Prix Tripoli*, p. 10.

"fastest road circuit in the world": *Motor Sport*, June 1935.

"[Mechanic] No. 1 gets the left rear wheel ready . . .": Neubauer, *Speed Was My Life*, p. 156.

"the secret of victory": Caracciola, *Rennen*, p. 83.

"There was the sun . . .": Caracciola, *Racing Car Driver's World*, p. 118.

"Well done, my dear boy . . .": Rao, *Rudolf Caracciola*, p. 210.

CHAPTER 16

"the great misery . . .": *La Vie Automobile*, July 10, 1935.

"When will it be understood . . .": *L'Intransigent*, June 25, 1935.

René spent so much time: *L'Auto*, August 1, 1935. The effect of the WW fuel prompted a big debate, and Alfred Neubauer even called a press conference to refute the claims.

"He drove like a madman . . .": Purdy, *Kings of the Road*, pp. 43–49. Purdy's book is one of the best chronicles of the Grand Prix world. It's well worth a read, and he is a delicious writer.

"Your name is Dreyfus . . .": Dreyfus and Kimes, *My Two Lives*, p. 120. Although said by a Vichy judge during the war, the sentiment was no doubt the same expressed earlier by such racist ideologues.

Despite this underlying: Evelyne Dreyfus, interview with the author.

If anybody (apart from Nuvolari . . .): Ribet, interview with the author; *Motor Sport*, January 1936; Stevenson, *Driving Forces*, pp. 138–50; Tragatsch, *Die Grossen Rennjahre 1919–1939*, pp. 259–60; Yates, *Ferrari*, pp. 108–9.

"racial disgrace": Don Sherman, "Porsche's Silent Partner," Hagerty, August 9, 2018, https://www.hagerty.com/articles-videos/articles/2018/08/09/the-story-of-adolf -rosenberger.

"They will decide . . .": Dreyfus and Kimes, *My Two Lives*, p. 87.

"splendid": *ACF Bulletin Officiel*, October 1935.

CHAPTER 17

With a jubilant shout: *La Vie Automobile*, February 25, 1936; *Club Delahaye Bulletin*, March 2002; Symons, *Monte Carlo Rally*, pp. 208–9; *Horizons*, March 1936; *L'Automobile sur la Côte d'Azur*, February 1936. Often, the Monte Carlo Rally was one of the most covered racing events of the season, with daily dispatches, many from the driver teams themselves, which provide incredible color to their progress across Europe.

"There you are . . .": Blight, *French Sports Car Revolution*, p. 151.

"The whole machine . . .": *Autocar*, September 1936.

"no longer be automobiles": *L'Auto*, February 15, 1936.

"the abyss": *L'Auto*, December 17, 1935.

"French prestige": *Paris Soir*, May 1, 1938.

"What is it now, Madame Schell?": Blight, *French Sports Car Revolution*, p. 175; Dreyfus, interview with Caron, DBA, 1973.

Over the next few days: Strother MacMinn, "Delahaye Type 145 Coupe," PPRA. In his essay about the development of the Delahaye Grand Prix car, MacMinn provides a wonderful glimpse into the creative process by Jean François—and the factors he and Monsier Charles considered were necessary.

CHAPTER 18

"It must be a drive . . .": *Autocar*, July 1936.

"thunderbolt known as Rosemeyer": *Motor*, June 1936. To read more about the incredibly gifted driver Rosemeyer—and his devil's bargain with the Third Reich—there are two very fine books: Frilling's *Elly Beinhorn und Bernd Rosemeyer* and Rosemeyer and Nixon's *Rosemeyer!*

"the fastest couple . . .": Cancellieri, *Auto Union*, p. 83.

"If [he] had not existed . . .": Pritchard, *Silver Arrows in Camera*, p. 161.

"the radiant boy": Day, *Silberpfeil und Hakenkreuz*, pp. 172–75.

"Beautiful blond Bernd": Ibid.

"Unforgettable, dazzling Bernd . . .": Ibid.

"German heroine": Ibid., pp. 175–83; Frilling, *Elly Beinhorn und Bernd Rosemeyer*, p. 67.

CHAPTER 19

"We still have a lot to do": *L'Intransigent*, December 18, 1935.

"Just go as fast as you can": Dreyfus and Kimes, *My Two Lives*, p. 64.

To design any car: In order to follow the progress of the Delahaye design, I also leaned heavily on two standard works, one specifically about the overall architecture of an automobile (Setright, *The Designers*), the other specifically about the V12 (Ludvigsen, *V12 Engine*).

"a peculiar pulse . . .": Ludvigsen, *V12 Engine*, p. 9.

"No wild innovations here": Strother MacMinn, "Delahaye Type 145," PPRA.

"finesse and intelligence": *L'Auto*, July 16, 1933, and May 10, 1936.

"who talked a very good story": Dreyfus and Kimes, *My Two Lives*, p. 70; Dreyfus, interview with Caron, 1973.

CHAPTER 20

"long walk": Dreyfus and Kimes, *My Two Lives*, p. 70.

By the time they arrived: *La Vie Automobile*, February 25, 1937; *Autocar*, February 5, 1937; *Motor*, February 2, 1937; *Motor Sport*, February 1937; *L'Auto*, January 24–February 3, 1937.

"Which way do you want to turn, René?": Dreyfus and Kimes, *My Two Lives*, p. 71.

"Bet that today . . .": *L'Intransigent*, January 24–31, 1937.

CHAPTER 21

"The Age of Sport . . .": *L'Auto*, August 1, 1936.

"Swift as greyhounds . . .": Day, *Silberpfeil und Hakenkreuz*, p. 137.

"Sheep in wolves' clothing": *Miniature Auto*, August 1966.

"as if this were a Grand Prix": Dreyfus and Kimes, *My Two Lives*, p. 76; *Motor*, June 22, 1937; *Motor Sport*, July 1991.

"brutal": Blight, *French Sports Car Revolution*, pp. 351–52; *Classic and Sports Car*,
    undated news clip, René Dreyfus Scrapbooks, MMA.
"How is she going to behave?": *L'Intransigent*, June 27, 1937.
As the V12 took life: Strother MacMinn, "Delahaye Type 145 Coupe," PPRA;
    Classic and Sports Car, undated news clip, René Dreyfus Scrapbooks, MMA.
"She's pretty, is she . . .": *L'Intransigent*, June 27, 1937.
"It was to catch the imagination . . .": Blight, *French Sports Car Revolution*, p. 289.

CHAPTER 22

"Make a perfect start . . .": *Motor Trend*, April 1975.
Production figures at Mercedes: Pohl, Habeth-Allhorn, and Brüninghaus, *Die
    Daimler-Benz AG in den Jahren*, pp. 134–47. Hitler decidedly followed through on
    his promises from the Berlin Motor Show in 1933, and it is remarkable how much
    success in motorsport fed an expanding German economy—and its rearmament. To
    read further on this, Reuss's *Hitler's Motor Racing Battles* is a fine book.
"Caracciola, the man without nerves": Day, *Silberpfeil und Hakenkreuz*,
    pp. 157–59.
"racetrack battle": Reuss, *Hitler's Motor Racing Battles*, p. 29; Day, *Silberpfeil und
    Hakenkreuz*, pp. 148–50.

CHAPTER 23

"In bars and cafés . . .": Blight, *French Sports Car Revolution*, p. 377.
"The engine turned . . .": Dreyfus, interview with Caron, 1973.
"It's very simple": Ibid.
"Ah, if I was ten years younger": *L'Auto*, August 24, 1937.
"Hesitant": Ibid.
"It's possible": Ibid.
"national interest": "Protokoll uber die am Donnerstag, den 28. Juli 1937," board
    minutes, 1.01 0021, DBA.

CHAPTER 24

"You must try tomorrow,": René Dreyfus, "Ma Course Au Million," reprinted in
    Club Delahaye Bulletin, June 2011.

"Who is it?": Dreyfus, interview with Caron, 1973; René Dreyfus, "Dotation du Fonds de Course," undated and unsourced, PPRA; Jolly, *Delahaye: Sport et Prestige*, pp. 144–46; Dreyfus, fiftieth anniversary speech, September 1993, *Club Delahaye Bulletin*. Dreyfus recounted this ruse in many ways over the years to many interviewers. This conversation is assembled from these four authoritative sources.

"You have our confidence": Dreyfus, "Ma Course Au Million," reprinted in *Club Delahaye Bulletin*, June 2011.

CHAPTER 25

It hadn't been the quickest start: *L'Auto*, August 27–September 15, 1937; *L'Intransigent*, August 29, 1937; Dreyfus, "Ma Course Au Million," reprinted in *Club Delahaye Bulletin*, June 2011; Dreyfus, interview with Caron, 1973; notes on interview with Dreyfus by J. P. Bernard. PPRA; Dreyfus, "Donation du Fonds de Course," undated and unsourced, PPRA; Dreyfus and Kimes, *My Two Lives*, pp. 81–82; René Dreyfus, letter to Martin Dean, June 14, 1985, René Dreyfus Scrapbooks, MMA; Blight, *French Sports Car Revolution*, pp. 381–82; Jolly, *Delahaye: Sport et Prestige*, pp. 145–47; Dreyfus, fiftieth anniversary speech, September 1993, *Club Delahaye Bulletin*. The author drew on scores of primary and secondary sources, including photographs from the Mullin Museum and elsewhere, to reenact the August 27, 1937, Million Franc run by René in fine detail. These are the chief sources the author used throughout the two sections recounting the events. Quotes and other critical material are noted separately.

Five minutes 22.9 seconds: *L'Auto*, August 28, 1937. All times and speeds are derived from tables published by *L'Auto*. To be completely accurate, René needed to run an average lap speed of 5 minutes 7.15 seconds, rather than simply 5 minutes 7 seconds, to beat 1 hour 21 minutes 54.4 seconds. Over sixteen laps, this small percentage difference makes over two seconds of difference in favor of the "deficit" René needed to win back. To avoid a trial in mathematics, the author rounded down the figures. Any errors are his alone.

In the seventh lap, the wind: Robert Puval, "Un Million pour Quelques Dixiemes," undated, unsourced news clip, René Dreyfus Scrapbooks, MMA; "A 210 Kilometeres a l'Heure René Dreyfus Lache le Volant," undated, unsourced news clip, René Dreyfus Scrapbooks, MMA. In these two articles drawn from the Mullin Museum Archives on René Dreyfus, the journalists recount rides on the Montlhéry track (one with René himself) that put the reader into the moment and conveyed how it felt.

CHAPTER 26

"Tomorrow morning . . .": *L'Auto*, August 29, 1937.

She had come to expect such slights: Lucy Schell, letter to Maurice Phillipe, May 5, 1938, Maurice Phillipe Papers, REVS. This remarkable letter to the editor of a major French publisher reveals the bitterness and hurt Lucy felt from the sexism that pervaded motorsport at the time.

"Were Bugatti and Wimille . . .": Blight, *French Sports Car Revolution*, p. 383.

At 4 p.m.: Dreyfus, "Ma Course Au Million," reprinted in *Club Delahaye Bulletin*, June 2011; *Le Journal*, September 1, 1937; *L'Intransigent*, September 1, 1937; Dreyfus, interview with Caron, 1973; Paris and Mearns, *Jean-Pierre Wimille*, pp. 121–23. This last-minute duel is well recounted in these sources, particularly the latter reference, which makes for a great introduction to Wimille.

"It's too late": *L'Auto*, September 1, 1937.

"Bravo! . . .": Paris and Mearns, *Jean-Pierre Wimille*, preface.

"driven like a god": *L'Action Automobile*, September 1937; Jolly, *Delahaye V12*, pp. 10–11.

"creator of Écurie Bleue": Dreyfus, "Ma Course Au Million," reprinted in *Club Delahaye Bulletin*, June 2011.

CHAPTER 27

At the airport outside Frankfurt: *Autocar*, November 5, 1937; Ludvigsen, *Mercedes-Benz Racing Cars*, pp. 140–43; Nixon, *Racing the Silver Arrows*, pp. 206–8. In attendance at the October record-breaking session, *Autocar*'s John Dugdale provides fascinating insight into the aerodynamic engineering of Mercedes. See also his book *Great Motor Sport of the Thirties*.

"We cannot go on this way . . .": Nolan, *Men of Thunder*, p. 180.

"Going on past form": *Autocar*, November 19, 1937.

CHAPTER 28

In Frankfurt, on January 27, 1938: Ludvigsen, *Mercedes-Benz Racing Cars*, pp. 151–53; Neubauer, *Speed Was My Life*, pp. 106–9; Caracciola, *Racing Car Driver's World*, pp. 121–25; Rao, *Rudolf Caracciola*, pp. 289–90; *Motor und Sport*, February 6, 1938. This description of Caracciola's record run is particularly indebted to his memoir and the account by Neubauer. All quotes and details come from the sources noted.

Off Bernd went with a scream: "Bericht Rekorde Frankfurt/Main," February 2, 1938, 428/3020, DBA; Aldo Zana, "A Roadmap for a Tentative Explanation of Bernd Rosemeyer's January 28, 1938 Accident," at the website The Golden Era of Grand Prix Racing, http://www.kolumbus.fi/leif.snellman/zana.htm; Caracciola, *Racing Car Driver's World*, pp. 125–28; Rosemeyer and Nixon, *Rosemeyer!*, pp. 179–82. Feuereissen wrote an evocative account of Rosemeyer's crash in Nixon's book. The Zana study is the most authoritative on what exactly happened that fateful January day. All quotes and details come from the sources noted here.

"A deadly misfortune . . .": Goebbels, *Die Tagebücher*, pp. 121–22.

"the news of your husband's tragic fate . . .": Frilling, *Elly Beinhorn und Bernd Rosemeyer*, pp. 321–22.

"chivalrous match": "Betr.: Rekordversuch," note between Hühnlein and Kissel, December 1, 1937, 12/25, DBA.

CHAPTER 29

"beloved child": *L'Auto*, February 19–22, 1938.

"over ten million Germans . . .": Kershaw, *Hitler*, p. 73.

"a state of ecstasy.": Shirer, *Rise and Fall of the Third Reich*, p. 334.

"Individual Jews were robbed . . .": Kershaw, *Hitler*, p. 84.

"The hard fact . . .": Shirer, *Berlin Diary*, p. 107.

"Britain and France . . .": Ibid.

"ten thousand scalded cats": *Motor Sport*, April 1938.

CHAPTER 30

"Every blow to Schmeling's eyes . . .": Frilling, *Elly Beinhorn und Bernd Rosemeyer*, p. 101.

Lucy may have said: Evelyne Dreyfus, interview with the author; Dreyfus and
Kimes, *My Two Lives*, p. 87; Ribet, interview with the author; *Auto Moto Retro*,
October 1987. Although we do not know the exact words between Lucy and
René during this last meeting, these sources convey how he understood Pau to be
greater than a simple race.

"find something to struggle and fight for": *Sports Car Guide*, September 1959;
Dreyfus and Kimes, *My Two Lives*, p. 51; *Automobile Quarterly*, Summer 1967.

CHAPTER 31

Nuvolari decided to see: *L'Auto Italiana*, April 20, 1938; *Il Littoriale*, April 9, 1938;
Moretti, *When Nuvolari Raced . . .* , p. 56. The loss of the Flying Mantuan at
Pau was devastating to its organizers—and widely covered in the press, almost to
the level of the race itself.

"the car into the lake . . .": *Automobile Quarterly*, 1st quarter 1937.

"This takes away . . .": "Betreff: Gross Preis von Pau, April 9, 1938," 1137/1, DBA;
"Telefongesprach Director Sailer aus Pau," 18.40 Uhr. 9.4.38, 1137/1, DBA. These
dispatches by Mercedes staff between Pau and Stuttgart provide incredible insight
into the opening of the new formula season.

"mastery of German engineers": "Mercedes-Benz Pressedienst, April 5, 1938,"
1137/1, DBA.

"Surely, Mercedes should win": *L'Auto*, April 10, 1938.

"The outcome of this race . . .": *Automobile Quarterly*, Summer 1964.

"beloved leader": Wilhelm Kissel, "Geleitwort zur Wahlhandlung am 10.
April 1938," March 31, 1938, 12.13, DBA.

"Hitler brought the German automobile industry . . .": Wilhelm Kissel,
"Deutschlands Automobile-Industrie dankt dem Führer," March 30, 1938, 12.13,
DBA.

CHAPTER 32

René Dreyfus paced his room: *L'Action Automobile*, May 1938; Dreyfus, interview
with Caron, 1973; *Automobile Quarterly*, Summer 1964; *Road and Track*,
December 1988; Darmendrail, *Le Grand Prix de Pau*, preface by René Dreyfus.
Thanks to these sources, I had a clear window into René's strategy—and fears—
on the night before the race.

"Are you in agreement . . .": Domarus, *Hitler*, p. 1089.

As 2 p.m. approached: Collection of news articles, ACBB Scrapbook. The hundreds of articles from French, German, Italian, and British newspapers that the ACBB collected in an oversize scrapbook for the Pau 1938 race provide much of the color/scene details included in my description.

"Five minutes": *Motor Sport*, June 1938.

"various dopes": Ibid.

CHAPTER 33

René released his clutch: *L'Auto*, April 11, 1938; Film of the reportings of *Éclair Journal*, Pau 1938, Gaumont-Pathe Archives; collection of news articles, ACBB Scrapbook; Dreyfus and Kimes, *My Two Lives*, pp. 85–87; *Motor Sport*, May 1938; *Road and Track*, December 1988; *Paris Soir*, April 11, 1938; Darmendrail, *Le Grand Prix de Pau*, pp. 57–64; "Telefonanruf H. Kudorfer 10.4.38," 15–18 Uhr. 1137/1, DBA; Lang, *Grand Prix Driver*, pp. 67–68; *Automobile Quarterly*, Summer 1964. Details over the next two chapters on the Pau Grand Prix 1938 were largely drawn from these sources. Any quotes or important details unique to a particular source are cited separately. Of especially good use were the internal Mercedes-Benz reports and the ACBB Scrapbook.

"paralyzing wheelspin": *Road and Track*, September 1988.

Rudi finished the first lap: ACBB, "Pau: Grand Prix de Vitesse: Report," 170/1137/1 1938, DBA. All lap times in the race are drawn from this ACBB report distributed to the press.

CHAPTER 34

"divine avenger": *Automobile Quarterly*, 2nd quarter 1980; *New York Times*, January 30, 1979.

"scientific driver": *Moteurs Course*, 3rd trimester 1956.

"There is little chance . . .": *L'Auto*, April 11, 1938.

"surpassed all my expectations . . .": *Paris Soir*, April 11, 1938; *New York Times*, April 11, 1938.

"right day, the right driver . . .": Jolly, *Delahaye V12*, pp. 12–13.

"One cannot congratulate . . .": *La Vie Automobile*, April 25, 1938.

"The success achieved . . .": *Paris Soir*, April 11, 1938.

"A Beautiful French Victory!": *Le Figaro*, April 11, 1938; *L'Auto*, April 11, 1938.

"There was something of a": *Automobile Quarterly*, Summer 1964; *Motor*,
   April 19, 1938.

"The first race run under . . .": *Motor Sport*, May 1938.

"dress rehearsal": "Telefonanruf H. Kudorfer 10.4.38," 18: 30 Uhr. 1137/1, DBA;
   "Telefonanruf H. Kudorfer 10.4.38," 20: 15 Uhr. 1137/1, DBA; German
   newspapers, as quoted in Herzog, *Unter dem Mercedes-Stern*, pp. 121–22.

"an embarrassing defeat": Nye and Goddard, *Dick and George: The Seaman-
   Monkhouse Letters*, p. 194.

AUTHOR'S NOTE

"Dreyfus was to the French people . . .": Dreyfus and Kimes, *My Two Lives*, p. 113;
   Auto Age, August 1956; *Autosport*, March 1, 1955.

"I've lived so many things . . .": Ribet, interview with the author.

"most beautiful cars in the world": André Vaucourt, article on the Delahaye V12,
   chassis # 48771, sent to the author.

"rolling sculpture": Sam Mann, interview with the author, New Jersey, 2019.

A debate has long simmered: Delahaye 145 Papers of Richard Adatto;
   correspondence between André Vaucourt and the author, 2018. It should be noted
   that homologation experts believe that the original chassis number assigned by
   the factory is the key to the puzzle, since neither of the chassis have suffered
   much alteration over the years. But if Delahaye or Lucy Schell maintained records
   about which chassis raced with which engine and body, at which race, they have
   been lost. Further, parts were often swapped between cars, and teams frequently
   doctored numbers and plates to avoid customs duties when traveling to races
   outside France.

"this life of fearful joys": Ferrari, *My Terrible Joys*, p. 13.

PHOTOGRAPH AND ILLUSTRATION CREDITS

INDEX

Note: Page numbers in *italics* refer to illustrations.

ACKNOWLEDGMENTS

As much as short and sweet is probably the best way to go in delivering acknowledgments, there is simply no way to do so with *The Racers*. I am indebted to many people around the globe who aided in delivering this history to readers.

First and foremost, Richard Adatto. He is a Delahaye and French coachbuilder historian, and since we were both living in Seattle at the time, he was one of the first people I reached out to, hoping he might have an insight or two. Our brief dinner turned into a long collaboration, which made this book richer far beyond measure. Richard opened up his extensive archives to me, offered introductions, provided research guidance, shepherded me through the Mullin Museum, and gave me a taste of what it was to drive the "Million Franc" Delahaye. He is a prince of a man.

In France, Jonathan Dupriez was my indefatigable researcher. He opened many doors for me and tracked down some obscure but key pieces of information about Lucy Schell and her family. Together, we toured some of the great Grand Prix racecourses of the 1930s. In Germany, Almut Schoenfeld, Marco Pontoni, and Maren Michel gave incredible assistance, helping to uncover the history of the Mercedes-Benz Silver Arrows and their links to the Third Reich. Thank you also to Almut for deciphering some texts for me that would have otherwise remained a mystery.

Finally, in the United States, Claire Barrett, Nicole Diehm, and Tatiana Castro hunted down numerous texts, magazine articles, and archives on my behalf. Their tireless efforts are greatly appreciated. My thanks also to André Vaucourt, a passionate, deeply knowledgeable expert on Delahaye who provided countless specifics on the French automotive firm from his own vast research.

Of the four Delahaye 145s built, collectors Peter Mullin and Sam Mann have cornered the market. They both met with me personally, shared their love of classic French cars, and generously gave me the opportunity to hear the roar of the V12 engine. Their passion for these race cars was infectious. Thanks also to Fred Simeone, who has his own treasures from the 1930s, in Philadelphia.

A big shout-out to Evelyne Dreyfus for providing me with a wonderful lunch and fond recollections of her father, Maurice, her uncle René, and the whole Dreyfus family. She also read an early version of the manuscript to make sure I had the story straight. Thank you for the many kindnesses, Evelyne. I also owe much to the pioneering research of Beverly Rae Kimes, co-author of René's memoir, a fine text in its own right. Her widowed husband, Jim Cox, shared the original audio recordings of Beverly's interviews with René. What a treasure. Jon Bill, curator of the Auburn Cord-Duesenberg Automobile Museum, which holds many of Beverly's archives, gave much assistance to plumb her original research as well.

Many, many folks illuminated for me the delightfully colorful world of the 1930s Grand Prix, shedding light on the master-pieces by Bugatti, Maserati, Mercedes-Benz, Auto Union, and Alfa Romeo and the characters who manufactured and competed in them. Thank you notably to Hervé Charbonneaux, Maurice Louche, Michel Ribet, Serge Bellu, Alfred Wurmser, Christian Schann, the late Pierre Darmendrail, Lydie Chiron, and Karl Ludvigsen. Special gratitude goes to Leif Snellman, who has probably collected more research into European racing in the 1930s than any other individual. His website The Golden Era of Grand Prix Racing is a must-have resource for any researcher of this period. Time and again, I drew from its pages.

As any historian knows, the dedicated efforts of librarians and archivists make possible our endeavors to bring stories of the past alive to readers. *The Racers* is no exception. Particular thanks to: Mark Vargas, director of the REVS Institute Library; Pierre Fassone, local memory Chatel-Guyon; Patricia Bourgeix for her tour of Montlhéry; the staff at the Daimler-Benz Archive, chiefly Gerhard Heidbrink, Wolfgang Rabus, Michael Jung, and Silvie Kiefer; the staff at the Automobile Club de Basco-Béarnais in Pau; Nathalie Verdino at the Automobile Club de Monaco; and André Gervais, archivist at the Automobile Club de Nice.

Two noted automotive enthusiasts, classic-car collectors, and generally knowledgeable fellows, Stephen Curtis and Flavien Marcais, were keenly helpful in guiding me to research, sharing their own, and, perhaps most important, combing through the first drafts to ensure that I did not mistake a carburetor for a camshaft, not to mention pointing out where I might have gotten the history wrong. Any errors, mistakes, or misunderstandings that remain are my burden alone to carry. Thank you, fine gentlemen. Carl Bartoli, my lovely father-in-law and engineer-on-call, was also helpful in making heads or tails of certain automotive systems, while also aiding with some important Italian-to-English translations.

Once again, I express my eternal gratitude to my publishing team at Scholastic for giving me the opportunity to share my passion for great narrative history to a younger audience. Nicholas Thomas first championed this project, and then Lisa Sandell stepped in to provide an incredible edit that made this book far better than it ever would have been in the first place. Masterful work.

As ever, my first line of defense, Liz Hudson, helped shape every paragraph and page. I'm lucky she still puts up with me after these many years. Finally, on my publishing team, nothing gets done without my agent, Eric Lupfer, who always has a wise word and a keen eye for what needs to get done.

Sam Walker and Christy Fletcher, longtime New York friends, set me on my journey to uncover the story of René Dreyfus, Lucy Schell, and the Delahaye 145. You two are the best, and that French chateau awaits your arrival.

Finally, as always, to my wife, Diane, and our two spirited daughters. I only wish life would go slower.

ABOUT THE AUTHOR

Neal Bascomb is the author of *The Nazi Hunters*, winner of the YALSA Excellence in Nonfiction Award, among numerous other awards. *School Library Journal* called his second young adult book, *Sabotage*, "excellent" in a starred review and *The Grand Escape* a "fantastic pick for avid history readers," also in a starred review. He is also the author of nine nonfiction books for adults on subjects ranging from a 1905 Russian submarine mutiny to a contemporary high school robotics team. *The Perfect Mile*, *Winter Fortress*, and *Hunting Eichmann* went on to be *New York Times* and international bestsellers. Neal lives in Philadelphia with his family and rascal dog, Moses. Please visit his website at nealbascomb.com and follow him on Facebook at @nealrbascomb.